Year 6
Workbook

Pearson

Published by Pearson Education Limited, 80 Strand, London, WC2R 0RL.
www.pearson.com/international-schools

Copies of official specifications for all Pearson Edexcel qualifications may be found on the website:
https://qualifications.pearson.com

Text © Pearson Education Limited 2023
Produced by Just Content Ltd
Designed by PDQ Media Digital Media Solutions
Typeset by PDQ Media Digital Media Solutions
Picture research by Straive Ltd
Original illustrations © Pearson Education Limited 2023
Cover design © Pearson Education Limited 2023

The right of Lesley Butcher to be identified as the author of this work has been asserted by her in accordance with the
Copyright, Designs and Patents Act 1988.

First published 2023

26
11

British Library Cataloguing in Publication Data
A catalogue record for this book is available from the British Library

ISBN 978 1 292 43340 0

Printed in Italy by L.E.G.O. S.p.A.

Contents

Micro-organisms

Micro-organisms are tiny living things. They are so small that we need a microscope to see them individually. Bacteria, viruses and microscopic fungi are all micro-organisms. We use some bacteria to make yoghurt and cheese, but others can harm us by causing food poisoning or disease.

In this topic we will learn:

- that micro-organisms can be bacteria, viruses or microscopic fungi

- to describe ways in which some micro-organisms can be useful, and others can be harmful

- about how micro-organisms grow and reproduce on food and some simple food hygiene precautions

- about the role of decomposers in food chains and the recycling of materials.

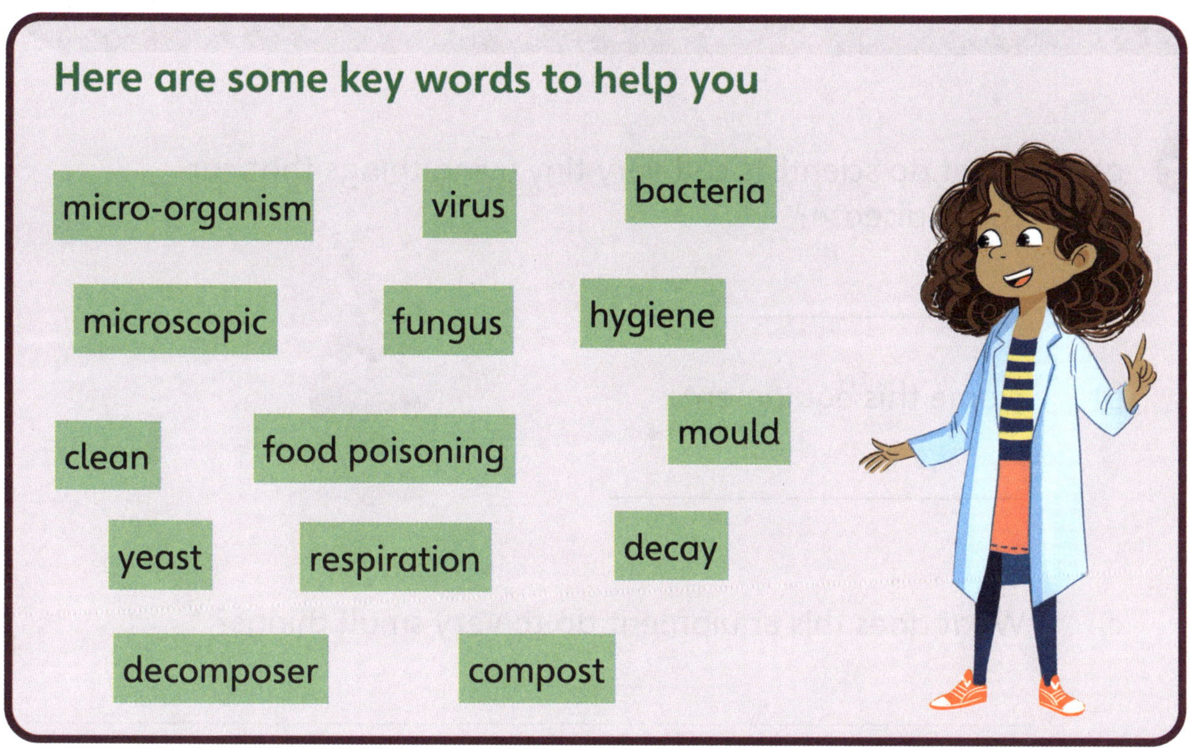

Choose two key words from the box above.
Write or draw what they mean.

What is a micro-organism?

1   a)   What do scientists call very tiny living things that can cause disease?

____

b)   Name this equipment.

____

c)   What does this equipment do to very small things?

____

2   Hundreds of years ago people did not know how diseases spread.

a)   Write **one** way they thought diseases might spread.

____

b)   Write **one** way we now know that diseases spread.

____

c)   Some people wear face masks like this today.

Suggest **one** way this helps to stop diseases spreading.

____

d)   What do we call a person who prescribes medicine for people who are ill?

____

3 Measles is the name of a disease caused by micro-organisms.

The information shows the number of young people ill with measles in one country during a three-month investigation.

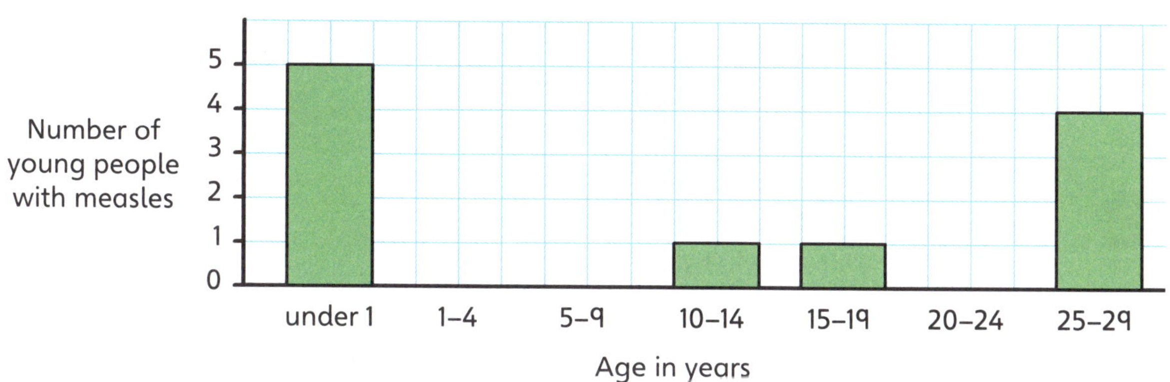

a) Two bars are missing.

Draw them using this information.

Age in years	Number of young people
1–4	2
20–24	3

b) There is no bar for 5–9 years.

What does this tell you?

____

c) In which age group were there **most** cases of measles?

____

d) In which age group were there 4 cases?

____

e) How many babies under 1 year old had measles?

1 Name **three** types of micro-organism.

1. _______________________   2. _______________________

3. _______________________

2 Complete the table.

a)   Name **three** diseases caused by micro-organisms.

b)   Name the type of micro-organism that causes each one.

Disease	Type of micro-organism that causes the disease

3 What type of micro-organism causes this foot infection?

____

4 a)   Find out **two** ways that someone would know they had food poisoning.

1. _______________________

2. _______________________

b)   What type of micro-organism causes food poisoning?

____

5 Many bacteria live in our digestive system.

a)   Draw some bacteria that live in our digestive system.

b)   Write about some of the things they do there.

Useful bacteria	Harmful bacteria

Food hygiene

1 a) What is happening to this orange?

____

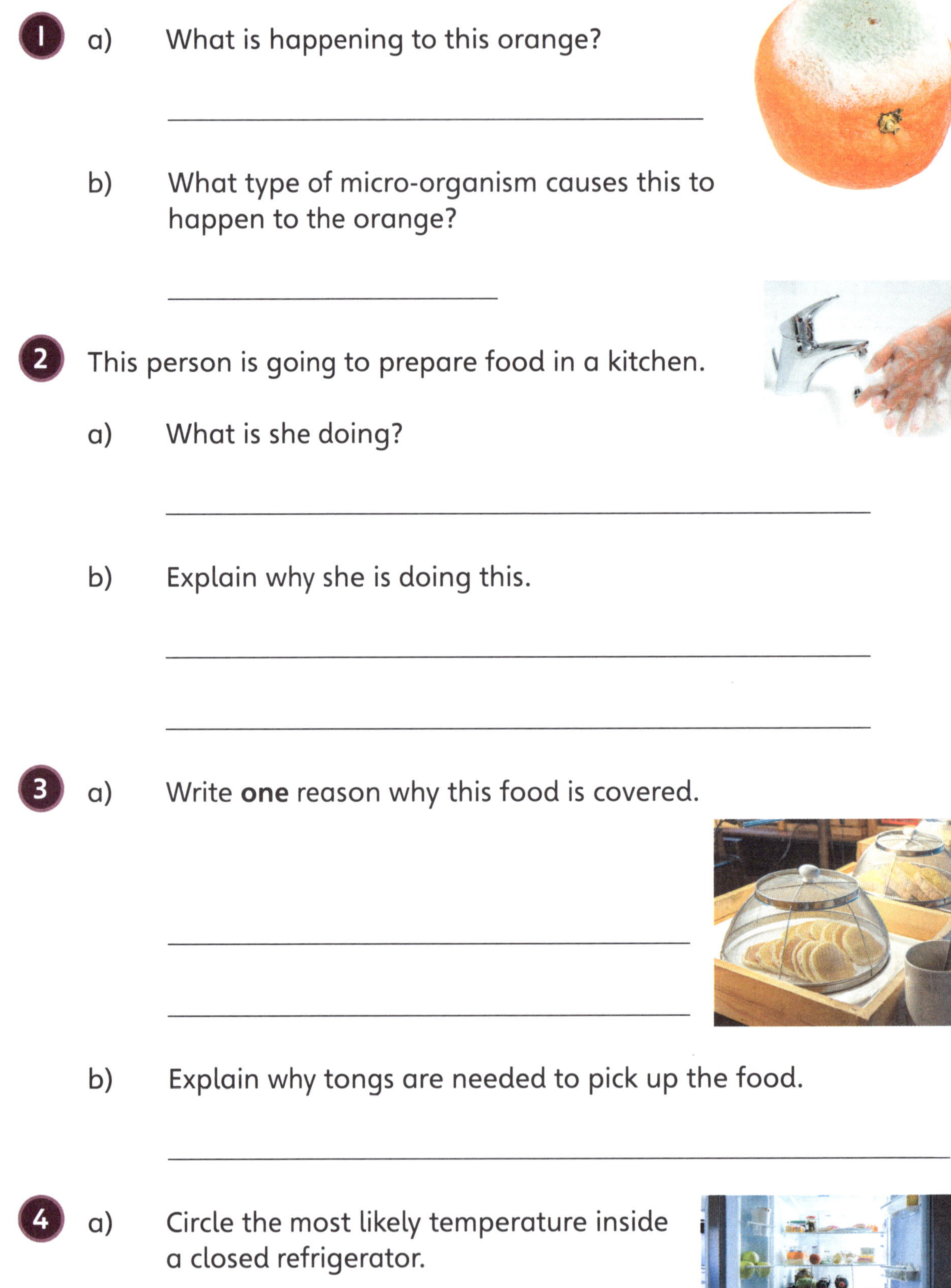

b) What type of micro-organism causes this to happen to the orange?

____

2 This person is going to prepare food in a kitchen.

a) What is she doing?

____

b) Explain why she is doing this.

____

____

3 a) Write **one** reason why this food is covered.

____

____

b) Explain why tongs are needed to pick up the food.

____

4 a) Circle the most likely temperature inside a closed refrigerator.

100 °C   52 °C   21 °C   4 °C

b) How does refrigerating food help to keep it safe to eat?

____

____

5 Someone who ate food from this restaurant kitchen became ill with food poisoning.

Write to the owner of the kitchen to tell them what they need to do to stop more people from getting food poisoning.

____

____

____

____

____

____

Mouldy bread

1 a) What is happening to this bread?

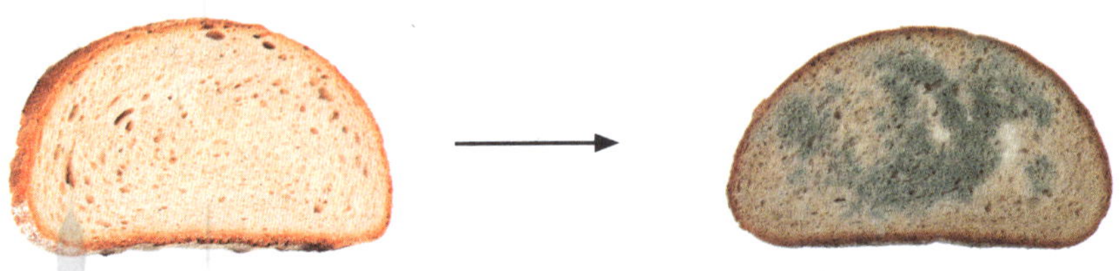

____

b) Circle the type of micro-organisms that made the bread change.

bacteria   microscopic fungi   viruses

2 Investigate the conditions needed to make bread go mouldy fastest.

a) Write your scientific question.

____

____

b) What will you change? Write in the first column of the table.

Conditions given to bread	Observations		
	Date:	Date:	Date:

c)   What will you observe and how often?

____

____

d)   (i)   Write the date in numbers at the top of the column each
             time you look at the bread.

      (ii)   Write what you see each time.

3 a)   Draw each slice of bread at the end of your third observation
             but do **not** open the bags.

<table>
<tr><td></td><td></td></tr>
<tr><td></td><td></td></tr>
</table>

b)   Write a conclusion that answers your scientific question.

____

____

c)   Suggest **one** improvement to your investigation.

____

____

Useful micro-organisms

1 Write **one** way in which micro-organisms can be useful and **one** way they can be harmful.

useful: ____

harmful: ____

2 a) Which type of micro-organism is yeast? Circle **one** answer.

bacterium   microscopic fungus   virus

b) (i) What do humans use yeast to do?

____

(ii) Explain how yeast does this.

____

____

____

3 a) Which type of micro-organism is used to make yoghurt? Circle **one** answer.

bacterium   microscopic fungus   virus

b) Draw some yoghurt and explain how it is made.

4

a) Name the **two** types of micro-organism used to make this blue cheese.

1. ___________________________

2. ___________________________

b) The arrows point to a vertical line in the cheese.

Suggest what happened here.

____

____

c) Draw **four** different cheeses that you or your family like to eat. If you do not eat cheese, choose some you see in shops or on television.

Write the name of the cheese under each picture.
Find out any names you do not know.

Decay

1 Write **one** word to describe what is happening to this fruit.

____

2 There are five words missing from the food chain below.

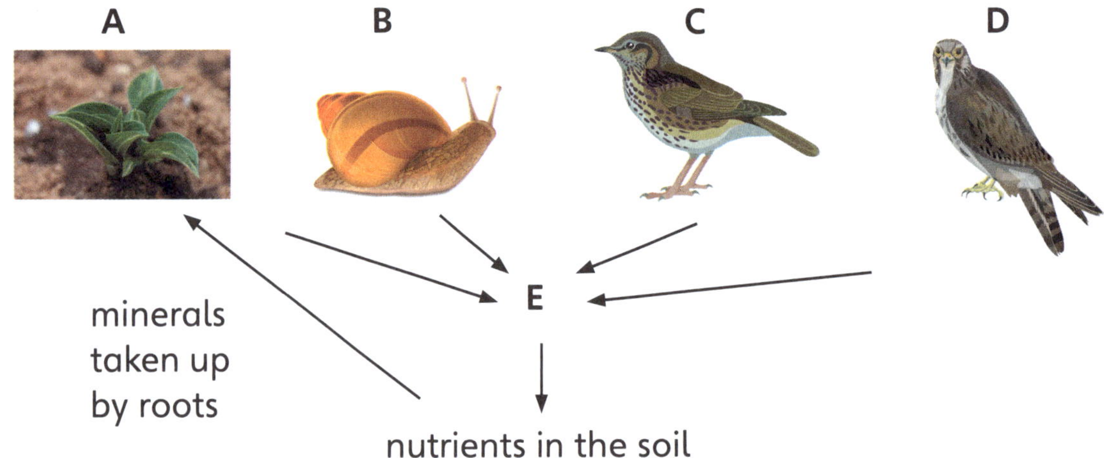

a) Write **one** word from the box beside each letter below. Use one of the words twice.

carnivore	herbivore	decomposer	producer

A _________________________   B _________________________

C _________________________   D _________________________

E _________________________

b) Name **two** types of micro-organism that are decomposers.

1. _________________________   2. _________________________

c) What do the decomposers in a food chain decay?

____

3 a) Predict what will happen to these dead leaves and explain how this happens.

____

____

____

b) Describe how to make compost.

    (i) Label things on the picture to help with your description.

    (ii) List some examples of what materials to compost.

____

____

____

    (iii) Write your description of what to do.

____

____

____

____

What have I learned?

1 I know the term *micro-organisms* and that these can be bacteria, viruses or microscopic fungi.

I know this because I can write **bacteria**, **viruses** or **microscopic fungi** on the correct rows of the table.

Yeast is one of these.	
E.coli is one of these.	
Influenza is caused by these.	
Mould is one of these.	
These are used to make yoghurt.	

2 I can describe ways in which some micro-organisms can be useful and others can be harmful.

I know this because I can write **two** ways in which micro-organisms can be **useful**.

1. ____

2. ____

I know this because I can write **two** ways in which micro-organisms can be **harmful**.

1. ____

2. ____

3 I can explain that micro-organisms grow and reproduce on food.
I can explain some simple food hygiene precautions.

I know this because I can write **four** different ways to make sure that food is safe to eat.

1. ____

2. ____

3. ____

4. ____

4 I understand the role of decomposers in food chains and the recycling of materials.

I know this because I can draw a food chain that includes decomposers.

I can also describe what decomposers do.

____

____

____

Plant life cycles

Plants have flowers so that they can make seeds. This is how they reproduce. To make a seed the flower must be able to move its pollen. It needs insects, other animals or the wind to do this. Many flowers are brightly coloured to attract insects and other pollinators, such as hummingbirds.

In this topic we will learn:

- that some plants have flowers, which produce seeds that grow into new plants

- how to identify the parts of an insect-pollinated flower and explain the function of each part

- what pollination is and the difference between insect and wind pollination

- the difference between pollination and fertilisation

- why seeds need to be dispersed and how this can happen

- about the conditions needed for seeds to germinate

- how to sequence the life cycle of a flowering plant.

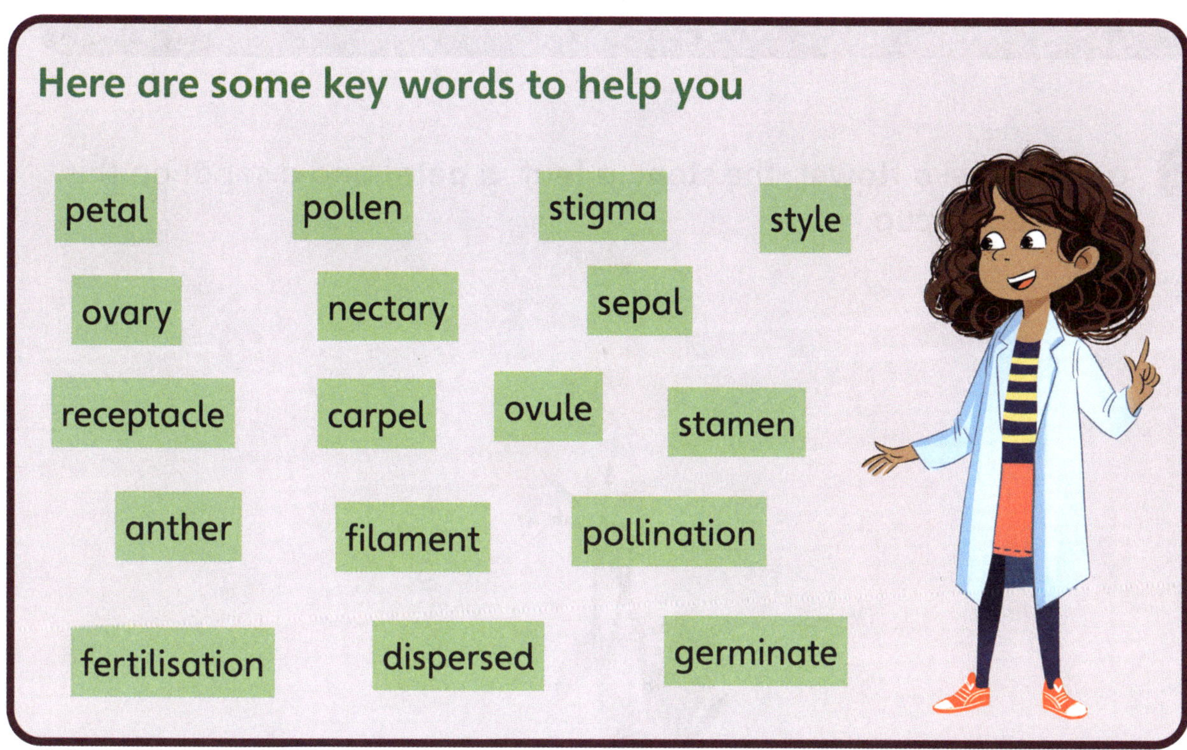

Choose two key words from the box above.
Write or draw what they mean.

Parts of a flower

1 a) Label a **flower**, the **stem**, a **leaf**, a **petal** and a **sepal** on this buttercup.

b) Circle **one** life process that plants need flowers to do.

movement   nutrition   reproduction   respiration

c) (i) What are these bees collecting?

____

(ii) Which part of the flower are they collecting this from?

____

2 a) The diagram shows parts of a flower. Name them all.

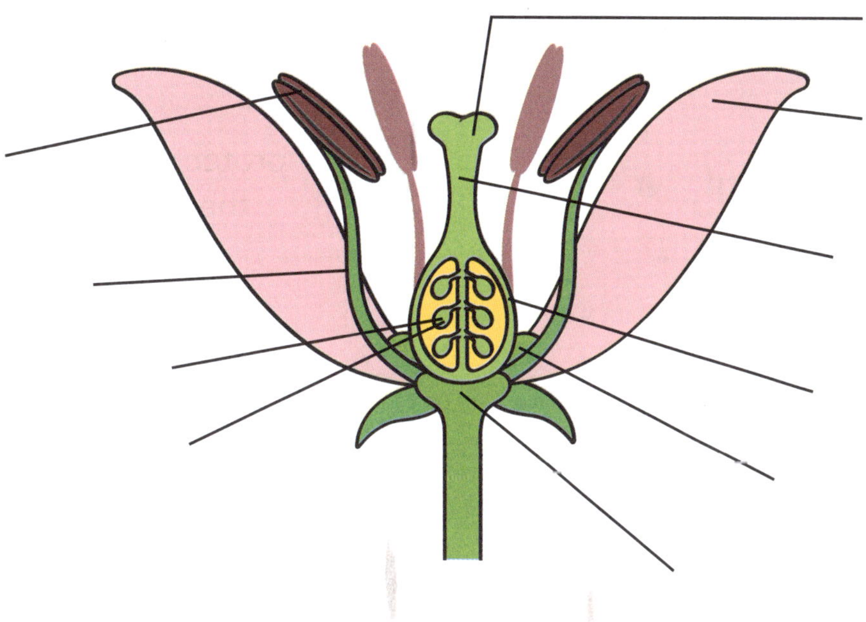

b) Name the **two** parts of a stamen.

1. ___________________________   2. ___________________________

c) The ovules are inside the carpel. Name **three** parts of a carpel.

1. _______________   2. _______________   3. _______________

3 The photograph below shows the centre of a lily flower.

a) How many stamens does it have?

b) What colour is the pollen?

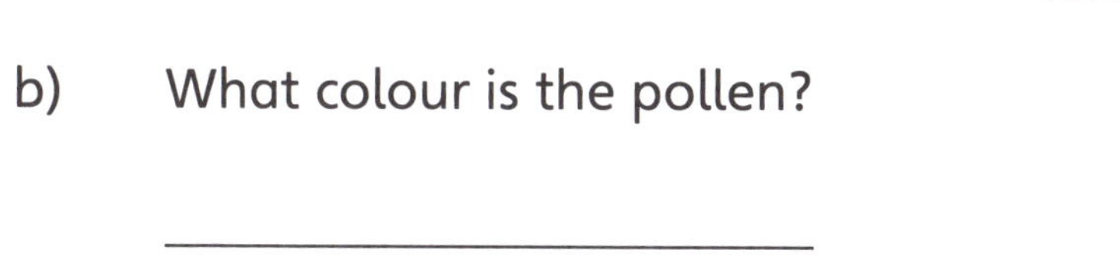

c) Draw the shape of the stigma.

Functions of parts of a flower

1 a)   Draw **one** line from each part of a flower to its function.

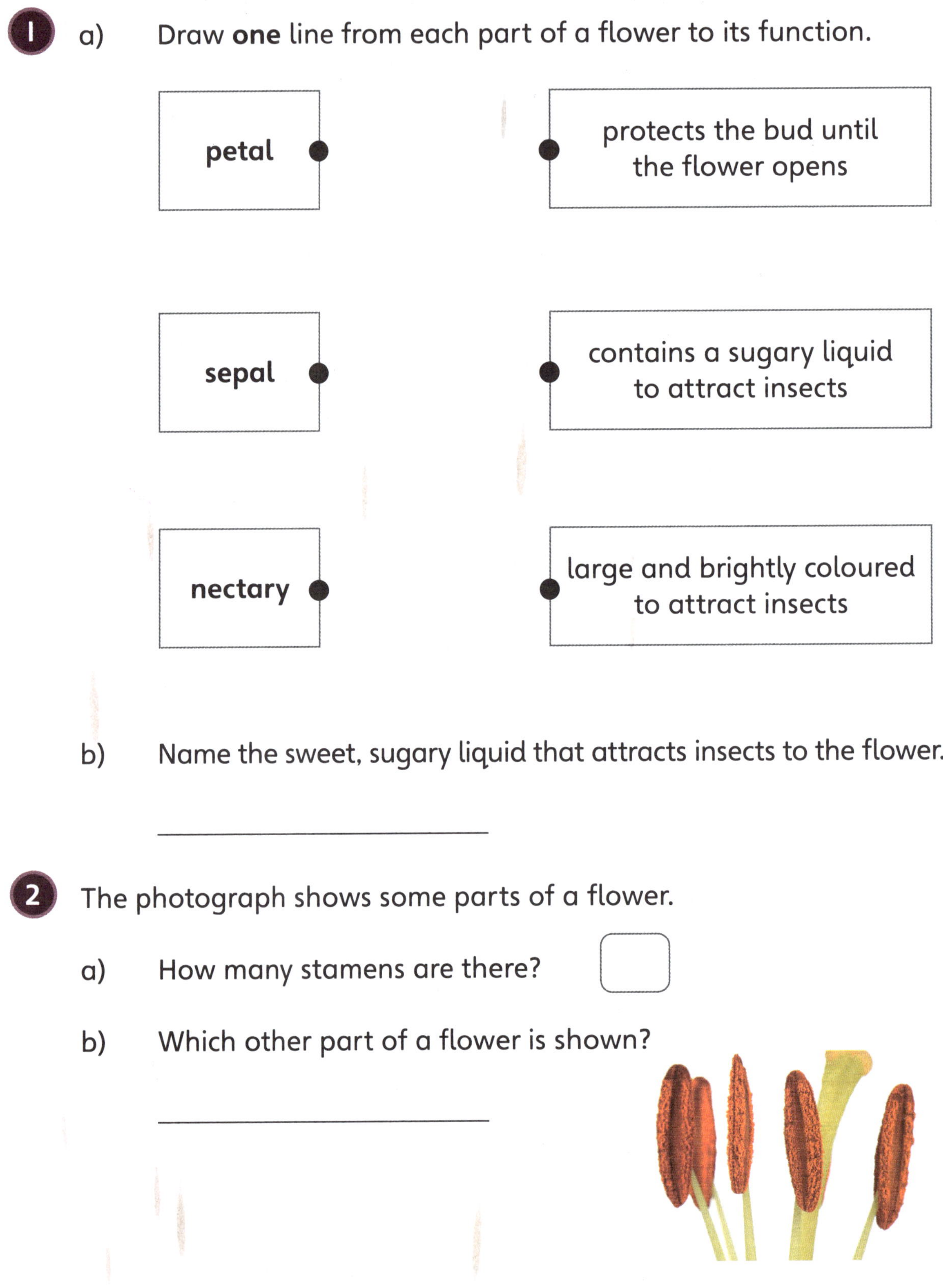

b)   Name the sweet, sugary liquid that attracts insects to the flower.

____

2   The photograph shows some parts of a flower.

a)   How many stamens are there?

b)   Which other part of a flower is shown?

____

3 a) (i) Complete the table by naming each flower part from its description.

(ii) Write **M** or **F** in the first column to show if each part you name is a **M**ale or a **F**emale part.

M or F?	Name of flower part	Description
		has a sticky surface for pollen to land on
		holds the stigma up and connects it to the ovary
		the wider part of the carpel containing the ovules
		these will later become seeds
		makes pollen
		holds the anther up and bends to brush pollen against insects

b) Name the flower part to which all the other parts are joined.

____

4 These flower petals have lines on them to help insects.

Suggest what the lines help insects to do.

____

____

Pollination and fertilisation

1   This bee is in a flower.

a)   What are the yellow dots on the bee?

____

b)   Which part of the flower made this yellow material?

____

2   The diagram shows one carpel that has been pollinated.

a)   Complete the **four** labels by naming the parts shown.

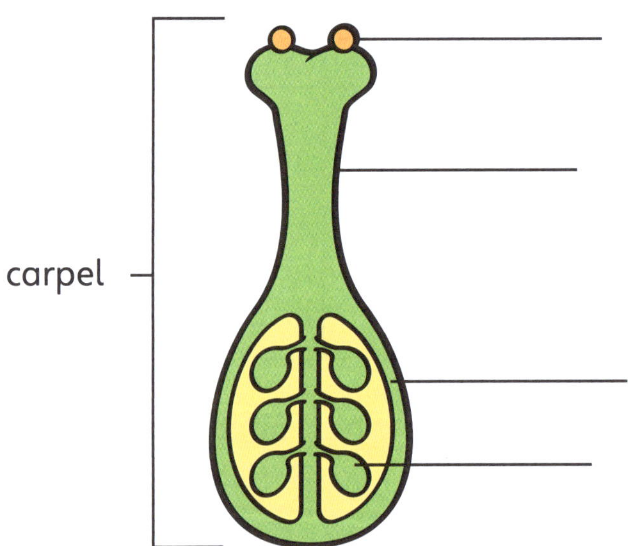

b)   Complete this sentence to describe pollination.

Pollination is the ______________________ of

______________________ from the anther to the

______________________ of the same flower or a

______________________ flower.

3 This diagram shows the same carpel later.

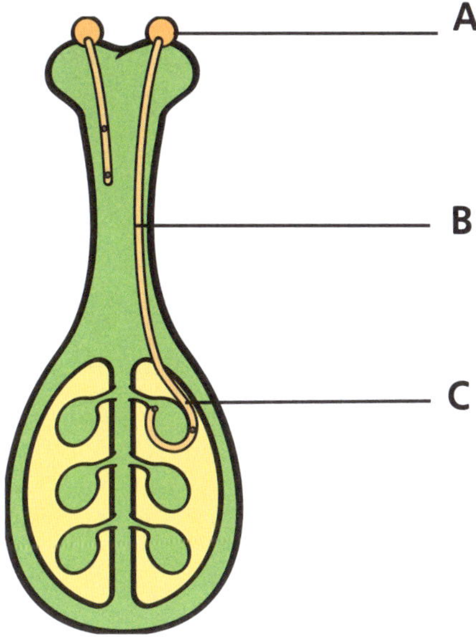

a)   (i)   Name **A** and **B**.

A _________________________   B _________________________

(ii)   Where is the orange tube turning to go to when it reaches **C**?

____

b)   Complete this sentence to describe fertilisation.

Fertilisation is when a nucleus from the male

_________________________ grain joins with a nucleus in

the female _________________________, which is inside the

_________________________.

c)   Each nucleus contains half the information to make something. What is being made?

____

Insect or wind pollination?

1　Draw **one** line from each flower to show whether it is insect-pollinated or wind-pollinated.

insect-pollinated

wind-pollinated

2 Hummingbirds and bats can be pollinators.

a) Explain what the word *pollinator* means.

____

b) In which part of a flower is pollen made? _________________

c) On which part of a flower must pollen land for the flower to be pollinated? _____________________________

3 The table shows some differences between insect-pollinated and wind-pollinated flowers.

Complete the table by writing **one** word in each answer space.

Insect-pollinated flowers	Wind-pollinated flowers
Bright flowers with coloured _______________ and nectar.	Flowers are small and often green.
Short _______________ so that the stamens are inside the flower.	Long _______________ so the anthers hang outside the flower.
Insects brush against sticky pollen inside the flower.	The _______________ blows small, light pollen grains.
Pollen carried by _______________ sticks to a stigma.	Long feathery _______________ hang out of the flower to catch wind-blown _______________.

Seeds

1. The photograph shows some dandelion seeds being dispersed.

   a)   Circle the part that is the seed.

   b)   How are these seeds being dispersed?

   ____

   c)   What does the word *dispersed* mean?

   ____

   d)   Seeds are dispersed to prevent competition with the parent plant. Write **three** things they might compete for.

   I.   _______________________   2.   _______________________

   3.   _______________________

2. This is a tomato flower and a tomato.

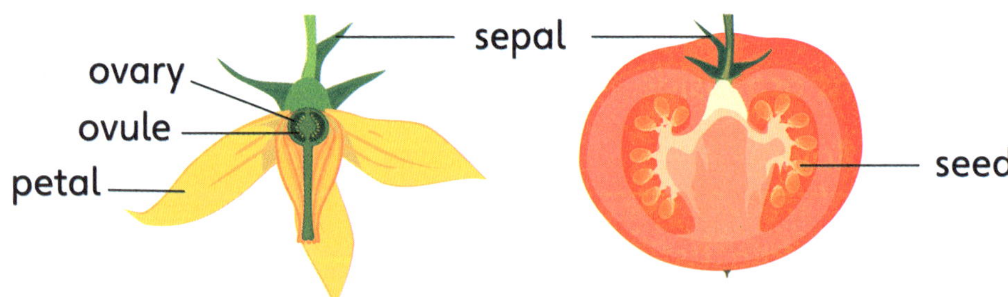

   a)   Name **one** flower part that you can see on **both** pictures.

   ____

   b)   Which part of the tomato flower becomes a seed?

   ____

   c)   Which part of the flower becomes the red part of the tomato?

   ____

3 Seeds can be dispersed in different ways. Complete the table by:

a)   writing **wind**, **water**, **animal** or **explosion** beside each picture

b)   describing how the seeds are dispersed by the method you chose.

	Wind, water, animal or explosion?	Description of what happens

Seed germination

1. This seed is starting to germinate.

   a) Complete the label by naming the part shown.

   b) Label the seed's **food store**.

2. a) Where does a germinating seed get water from?

   ____

   b) Which gas from the air do germinating seeds use for respiration?

   ____

3. Plan an investigation to show that seeds need water and air to germinate. Use **three** groups of seeds.

   a) Write your scientific question.

   ____

   ____

   b) (i) What type of seeds are you using? ___________________

   (ii) How many seeds will you put in each group?

   c) (i) Draw your three groups of seeds in the test tubes on the next page.

   (ii) Draw the other things you are putting in each tube.

   (iii) Write **one** of these under each tube:

water and air	no air	no water

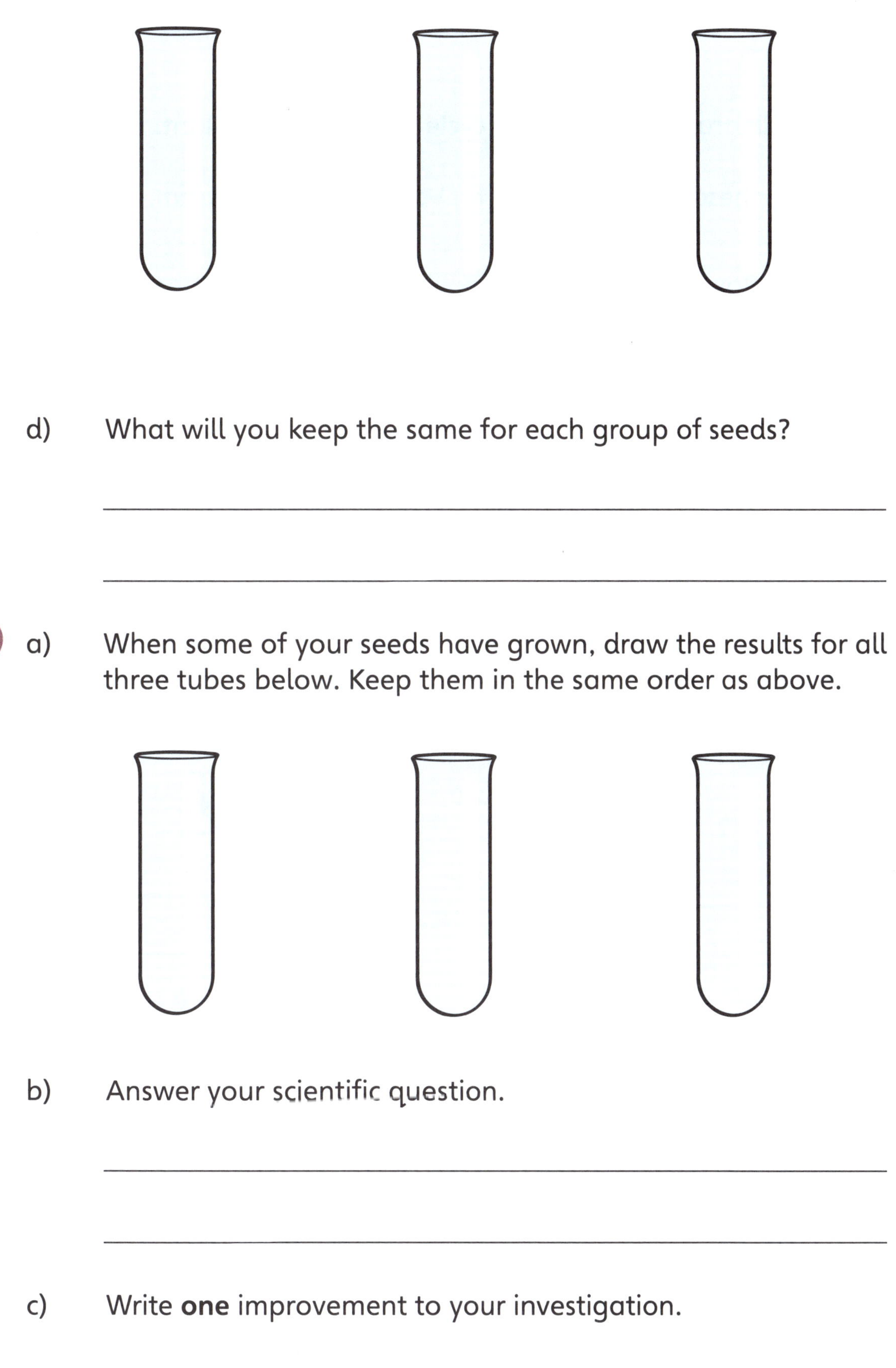

d) What will you keep the same for each group of seeds?

____

____

4 **a)** When some of your seeds have grown, draw the results for all three tubes below. Keep them in the same order as above.

b) Answer your scientific question.

____

____

c) Write **one** improvement to your investigation.

____

____

The life cycle of a flowering plant

The diagram shows the life cycle of a flowering plant.

Write these words in the correct place on the diagram.

flowering	pollination	germination
seed dispersal	growth	fertilisation

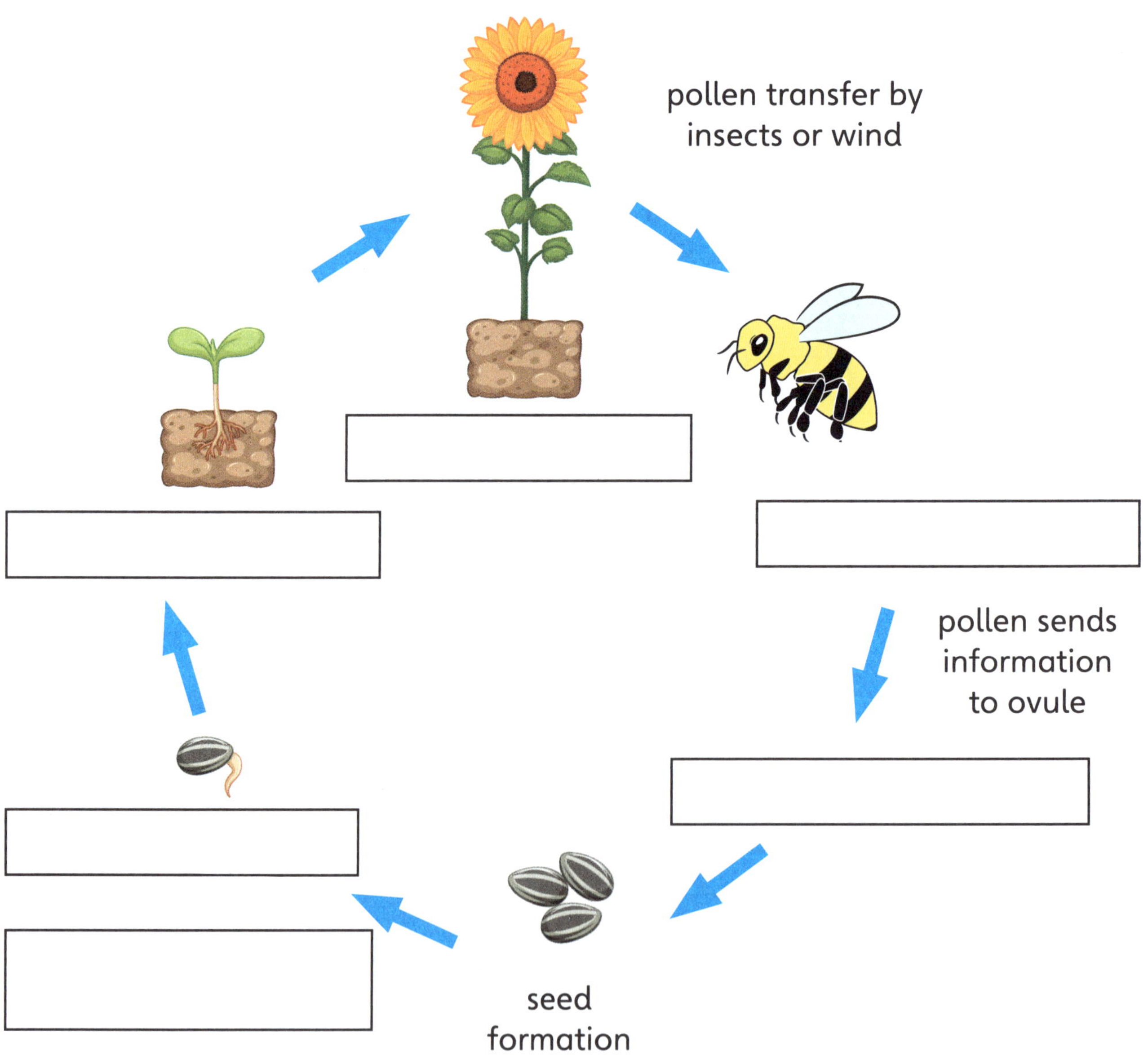

2 Some plants do not have flowers.

Write **flowers**, **cones** or **neither** under each picture.

What have I learned?

1 I understand that some plants have flowers, which produce seeds that grow into new plants.

I know this because I can name:

a flowering plant: _______________________

a non-flowering plant: _______________________

2 I can identify the parts of an insect-pollinated flower and explain the function of each part.

I know this because I can label **eight** different parts of this flower and tell my teacher or my partner their function.

3 a)   I know what **pollination** is.

I can draw a pollen grain on the flower above to show what pollination is.

b)   I know the difference between insect and wind pollination.

I know this because I can write **two** ways that wind-pollinated flowers differ from the flower in Question 2.

1. ____

2. ____

4 I know the difference between **pollination** and **fertilisation**.

Pollination is ____

____

Fertilisation is ____

____

5 I can explain why seeds need to be dispersed and can describe some different ways this can happen.

I know this because I can write **two** different ways that seeds can be dispersed.

1. __________________________   2. __________________________

6 I understand the conditions needed for seeds to germinate.

I know this because seeds need ________________ from the air and

______________________ from the soil as well as the correct temperature.

7 I know these words and the order of these stages in the life cycle of a flowering plant:

flowering	1		pollination			fertilisation	
germination			seed dispersal				

I know this because I can finish numbering them above.

Heart, lungs and circulation

Our heart and lungs are organs. Our lungs take air in and out of our bodies. This is breathing. Our blood takes the oxygen to all parts of our body in blood vessels. The heart pumps day and night to keep the blood moving.

In this topic we will learn:

- that the heart is an organ that pumps blood as part of the circulatory system

- that the circulatory system is the heart and blood vessels containing blood

- about how pulse rate changes with exercise

- that the lungs are in the thorax and are the organs used for breathing

- that air is a mixture of gases, including oxygen

- that blood picks up oxygen from the lungs and transports it through blood vessels to organs of the body

- to distinguish between and correctly use the terms 'breathing' and 'respiration'.

Choose two key words from the box above.
Write or draw what they mean.

The circulatory system

1 a) (i) Name this organ.

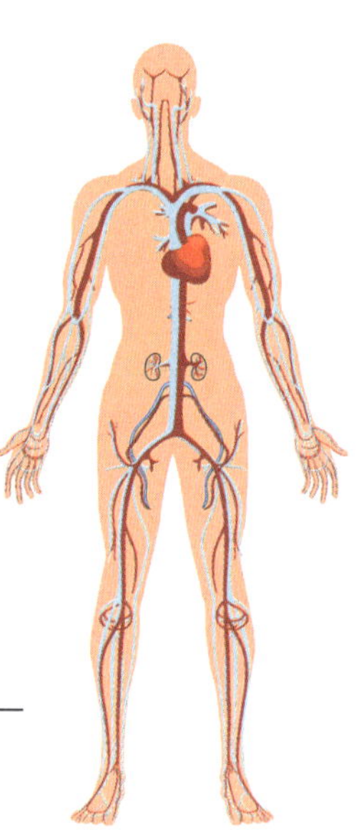

____

(ii) Name the liquid that it pumps around the body.

____

(iii) Circle this organ on the diagram of the circulatory system.

b) What are the coloured lines on the diagram of the circulatory system?

____

2 Diagrams **A** and **B** show two other body systems.

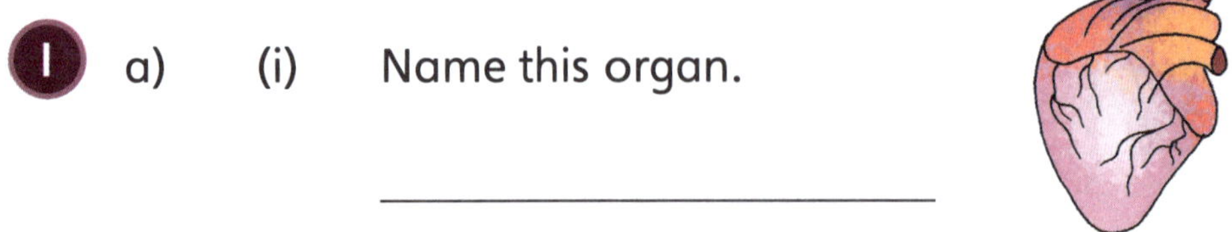

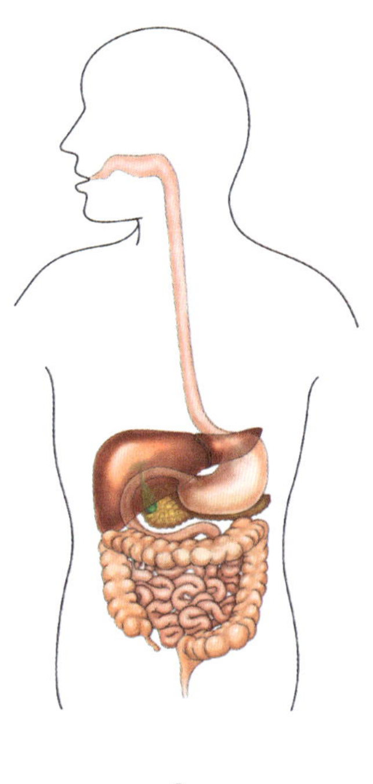

A

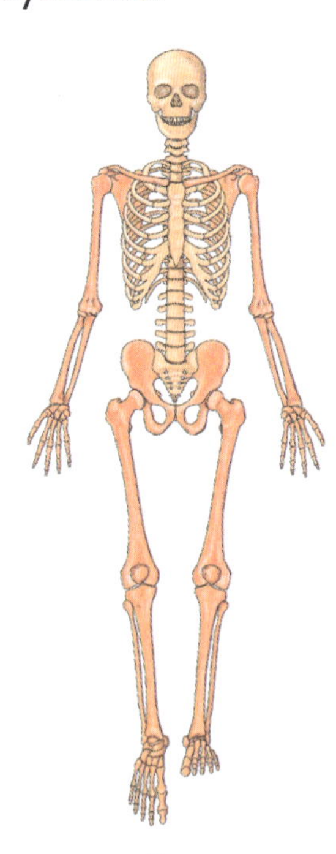

B

a) (i) Label the stomach on diagram **A**.

(ii) Label the skull on diagram **B**.

b)	(i)	Name the part of diagram **B** that protects the heart.

____

(ii)	Label this part on diagram **B**.

c)	Name the two systems shown in diagrams **A** and **B**.

Diagram **A** shows the ____________________ system.

Diagram **B** shows the ____________________ system.

3	The heart is a muscle that pumps blood.

a)	Write two opposite words that describe what muscles can do.

Muscles can __________________ or they can _________________.

b)	What special property does heart muscle have?

____

4	Use a stopwatch or a clock with seconds. Feel your heart beating. Count how many times it beats in one minute.

a)	(i)	How many times did you feel your heart beating in one minute?

There were [ ] beats in one minute.

(ii)	Repeat this count two more times.

First repeat: [ ] beats in one minute

Second repeat: [ ] beats in one minute

b)	Why is it important to repeat the counting?

____

What does the heart do?

I The diagram shows a heart and blood vessels. Use it to help you complete the sentence in a) and for the labels in b) and c).

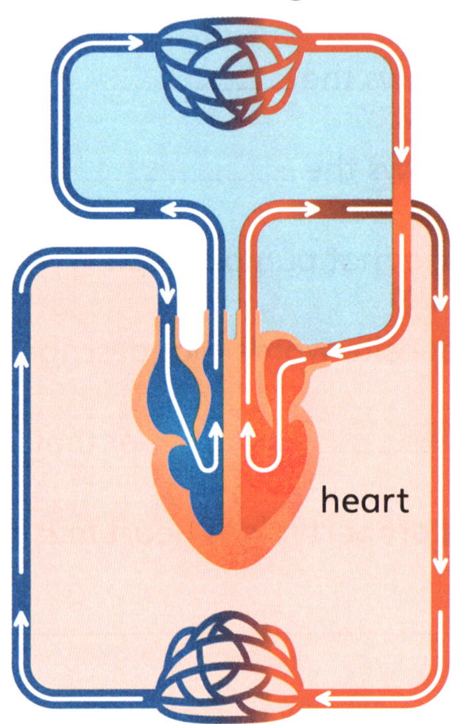

a) The heart pumps blood to the ________________________ and

to all other parts of our ________________________.

b) (i) Write letter **A** beside a blood vessel that is **taking blood to the** lungs.

(ii) Write letter **B** beside a blood vessel that is **taking blood away from the lungs**.

c) (i) Write letter **C** beside a blood vessel that is **taking blood to the body**.

(ii) Write letter **D** beside a blood vessel that is **taking blood away from the body**.

2 a) Name **three** things that blood takes to all parts of our body. The first letters are given.

o_______________________

n_______________________

w_______________________

b) Which part of the blood makes it look red?

____

c) Look at the pictures of blood vessels in your textbook. Look at the blood vessels on your arm.

Draw and write a description of blood vessels.

____

____

____

____

____

Investigating pulse rate

1 This screen shows information about a person who is lying on a hospital bed.

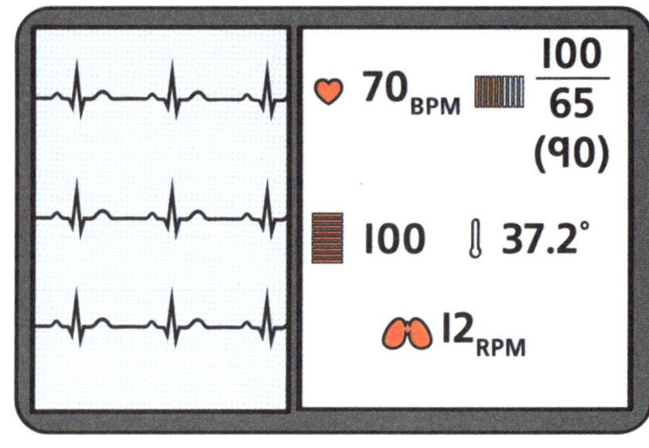

a) (i) What is this person's heart rate?

____

(ii) How did you decide which number was heart rate?

____

b) There is not enough room on the screen to write the temperature unit correctly.

Write this person's temperature, showing the unit correctly.

____

c) Predict what will happen to this person's pulse rate if they:

sit up in bed _______________________

walk up some stairs _______________________

2 Do the pulse rate investigation described in your textbook.

a) Record your results in this table in beats per minute.

Type of activity	Pulse rate in beats per minute			
	1st count	2nd count	3rd count	Average (mean)
sitting				
standing				
after exercise				

b)   Why did you count three times for each activity?

____

c)   Draw a bar graph for your results. Use only the mean averages rounded to the nearest whole number.

    (i)   Number the squares on the vertical axis 0, 20, 40, 60 as high as you need to go. Label the vertical axis.

    (ii)   Draw your bars three squares wide, with one square between them. Label the horizontal axis.

d)   Describe the pattern in your results.

____

____

The respiratory system

1 a) Name these **three** structures found in the chest.

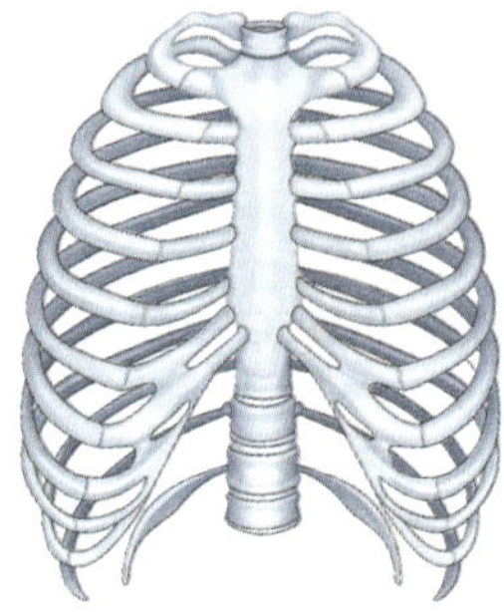 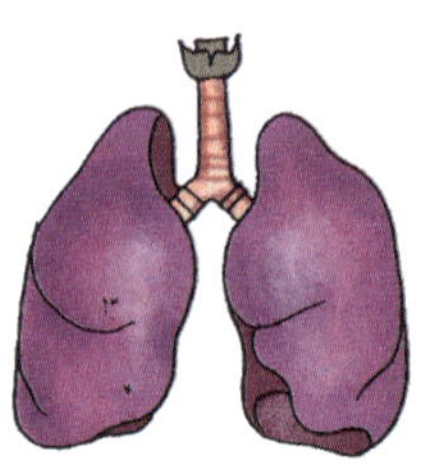 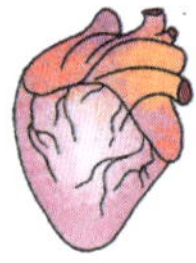

________________ ________________ ________________

b) Use a line and the word to label the **trachea** on one of the pictures.

2 The diagram shows what happens when we breathe in.

a) Name parts **1** and **2** in the boxes.

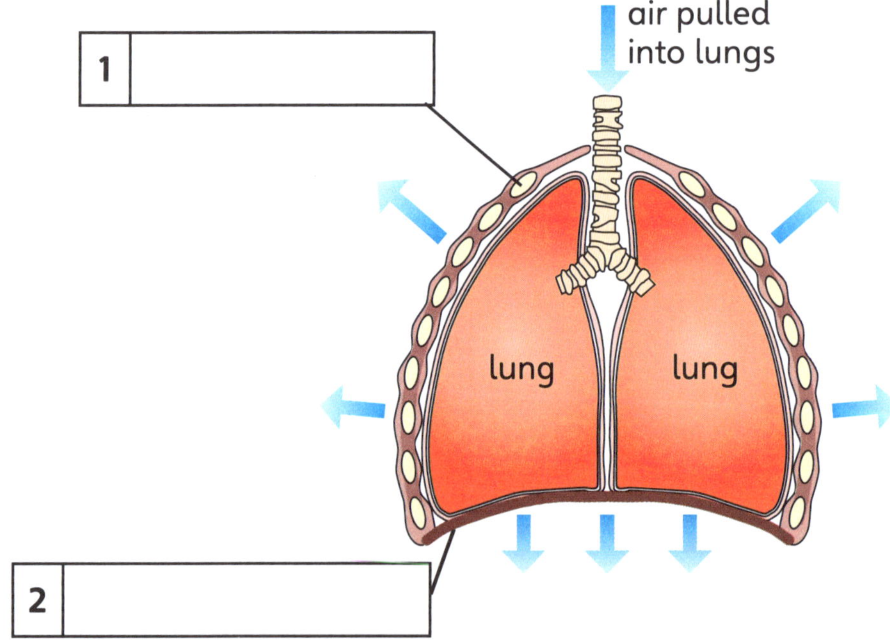

b) What materials are part **1** and part **2** made of?

Part **1** is made of ________________________ .

Part **2** is made of ________________________ .

c)   Describe how part **1** and part **2** move when we breathe in.

Part **1** ____

Part **2** ____

d)   Complete the sentences about breathing in.

When parts **1** and **2** move, it makes more space inside the

________________________.

Air is pulled ________________________ to fill this space.

Air enters through a tube called the ________________________.

e)   This diagram shows what happens when we breathe out.

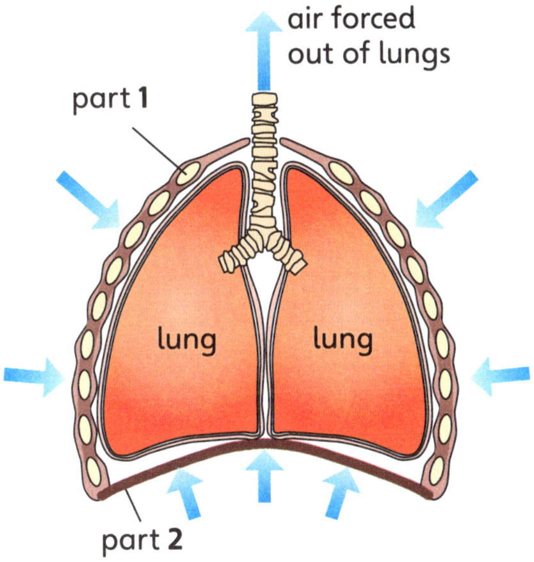

Describe what happens when we breathe out.
Start with how parts **1** and **2** move.

____

____

____

____

Modelling breathing

1. A learner makes this model of the human thorax using a big glass jar and some balloons.

   a) Use words from the box to label what **three** parts of the model represent.

   left lung   rib cage   trachea

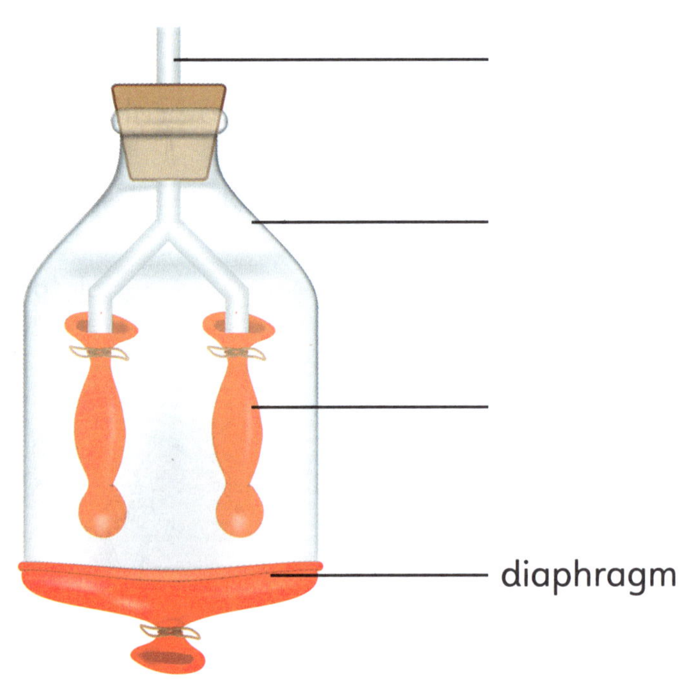

   b) How does the glass jar differ from a real rib cage?
      Write **three** different ways.

      1. ____

      ____

      2. ____

      ____

      3. ____

      ____

c)   The learner pulls the bottom balloon downwards.

    (i)   Draw what happens to the two balloons inside the glass jar.

    (ii)   When the learner pulls the bottom balloon down, how does this change the volume of the space inside the model?

    ____

    (iii)   Draw arrows on the diagram to show the pathway of air into the model lungs.

d)   Predict what will happen when the learner lets go of the bottom balloon.

____

e)   In a real body, what is the diaphragm made of?

____

2   Complete the sentences to give a definition of breathing.

Breathing is the word we use for taking _____________ in and _____________ of the lungs.

Breathing is sometimes called _____________________________ the lungs.

What happens to the air we breathe in?

1. Air is a mixture of gases. Which gas do we need to breathe in?

   ____

2. The diagram shows air entering the lungs. Use it to help you answer the questions.

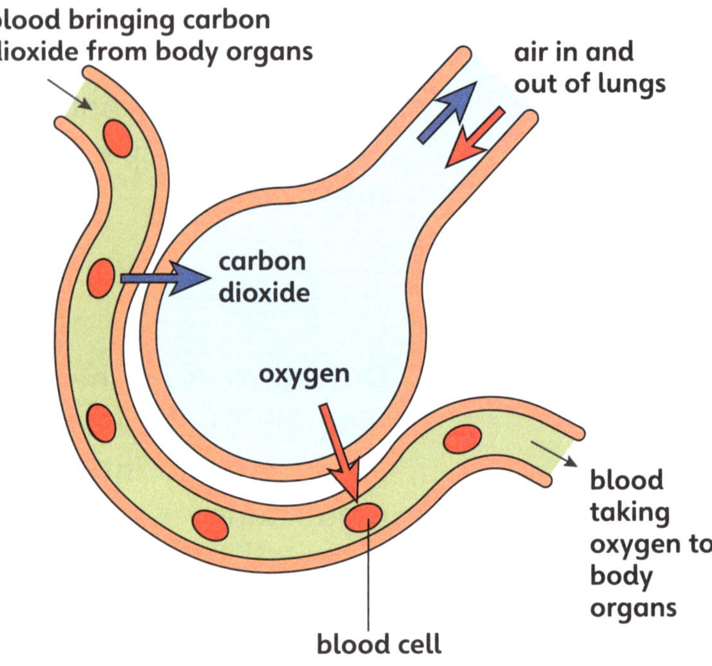

   a) Which organs do we use for breathing?

      ____

   b) What part of our skeleton protects our lungs?

      ____

   c) (i) Which gas does blood take to body organs?

      ____

   (ii) Which gas does blood bring back from body organs?

      ____

   d) Which organ pumps blood around our body?

      ____

3 The diagram shows blood going to a muscle. Use it to help you answer the questions.

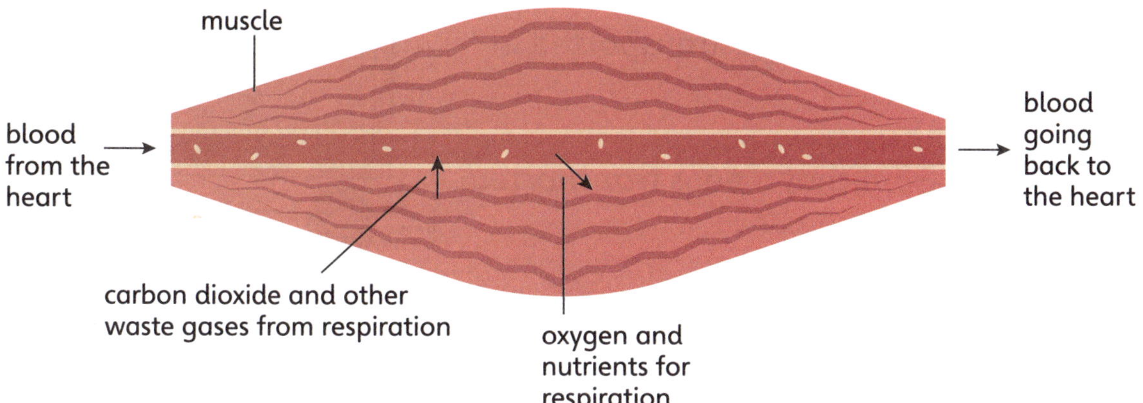

a) (i) Name **two** substances that blood brings for muscles to use.

I. _________________________   2. _________________________

(ii) Name **two** other places in the body that also need these substances.

I. _________________________   2. _________________________

b) For which life process do muscles need oxygen?

____

c) (i) Name **one** gas that muscles put back into the blood with their other waste.

____

(ii) How do we remove this waste gas from our body?

____

____

4 Complete the sentence to write a definition of respiration.

Respiration is how the body uses _________________________ when it reaches our organs.

Transport in our bodies

1 These substances are transported in our bodies.

Circle a word that means *transported*.

emptied   lost   mixed   moved   seen

2 a) The diagram shows parts of the circulatory system. Use it to help you answer the questions.

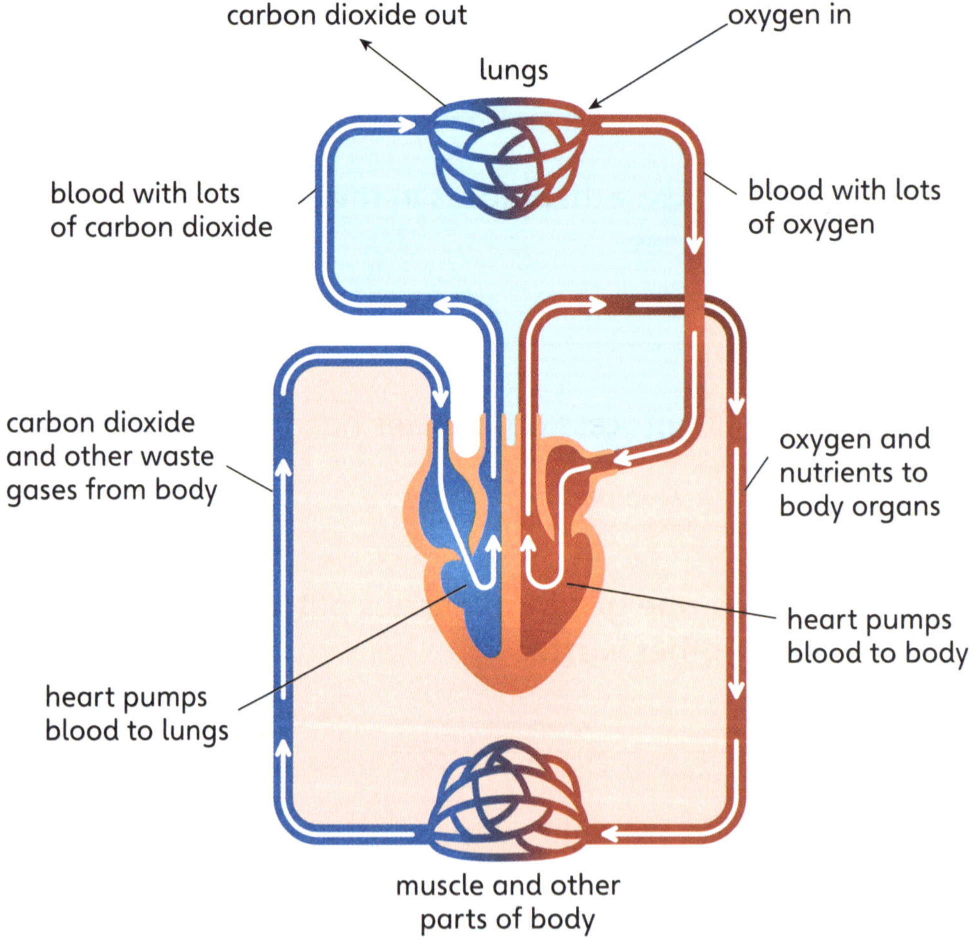

(i) What keeps blood moving around the body?

____

(ii) In what does blood travel round the body?

____

b) The table shows where three substances enter the blood. Complete the table to show where blood takes each substance.

Name of substance	Enters the blood at ...	Blood takes it to ...
oxygen	lungs	
nutrients	small intestine	
carbon dioxide	muscles and body organs	

c) Blood goes through the heart twice. Complete the diagram below to show this. Draw two more arrows.

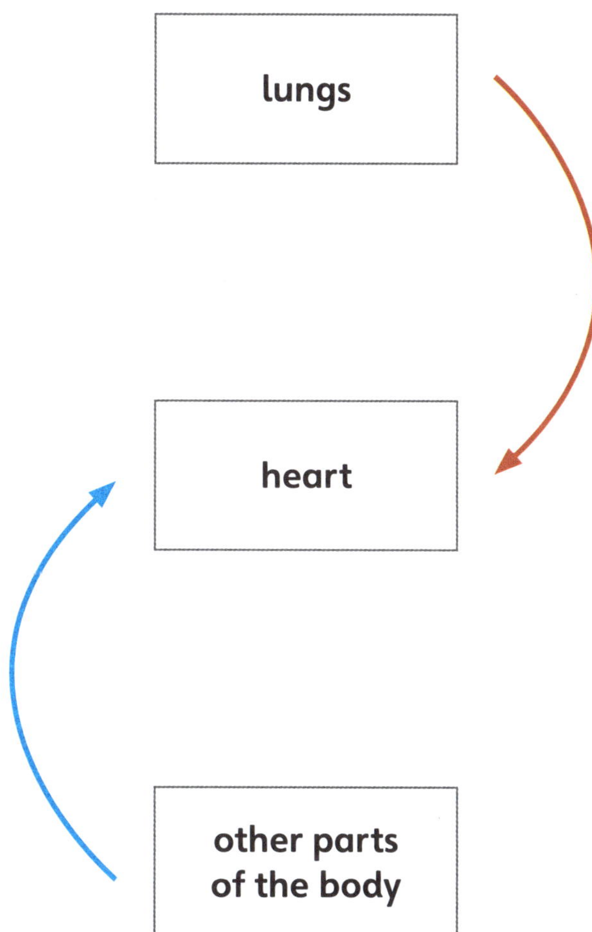

What have I learned?

1 I can describe the heart as an organ that pumps blood as part of the circulatory system.

I can describe the circulatory system as the heart and blood vessels containing blood.

I know this because I can circle the picture of the heart.

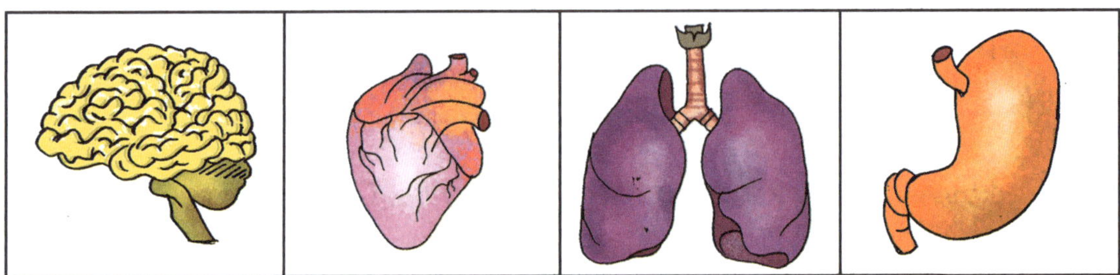

2 I understand how pulse rate changes with exercise.

I can explain the reason for the change because I understand that water and nutrients are transported around our bodies in blood.

I know this because I can describe how my pulse rate changes when I sit, then I exercise and then I sit again.

- When I sit my pulse rate is [   ] beats per minute.

- Immediately I stop exercising my pulse rate is [   ] beats per minute.

- After I stop exercising and I sit down for three minutes, my pulse rate is [   ] beats per minute.

This is because my muscles need _________________ and _________________ to be able to contract when I exercise.

3 I can describe the lungs as being in the thorax and as the organs used for breathing.

I know this because I can draw the position of the lungs on this diagram.

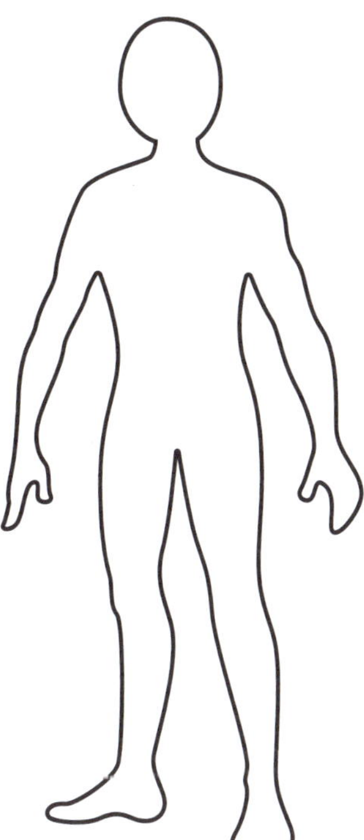

4 I understand that air is a mixture of gases, including oxygen.

I also understand that blood picks up oxygen from the lungs and transports it through blood vessels to organs of the body.

I know this because I can label a blood vessel on this diagram of a muscle.

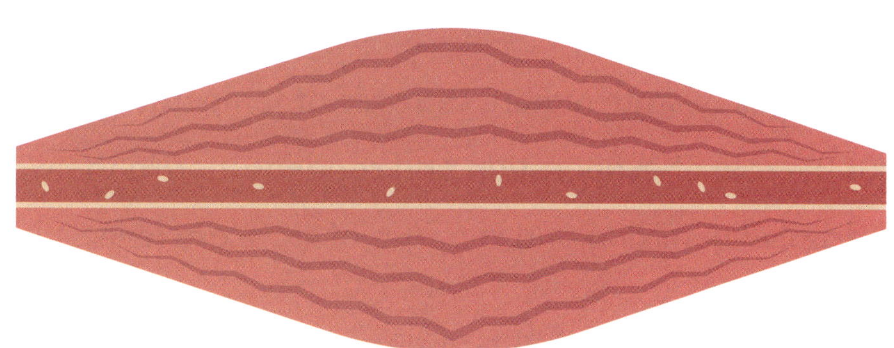

5 I can distinguish between and correctly use the terms *breathing* and *respiration*.

I know this because I can write each of these words beside the correct definition.

	how oxygen is used by the body once it reaches organs
	ventilation of the lungs

Reversible and irreversible change

If you mix sand and water, the sand does not dissolve so you can separate it from the water by filtration. A solution of salt and water can be separated by evaporating the water. When ice melts you can freeze it again. Each of these changes is reversible. Not all changes can be reversed.

In this topic we will learn:

- that mixtures can be separated using a sieve or filter

- how a solute can be recovered from a solution, using the terms *dissolving*, *solution*, *solvent* and *solute*

- that melting, freezing, evaporation and condensation are changes of state

- that changes of state require changes of temperature

- about the role of evaporation and condensation in the water cycle

- that dissolving, mixing and changes of state are reversible changes

- to describe simple irreversible changes and explain that these changes result in the formation of new materials.

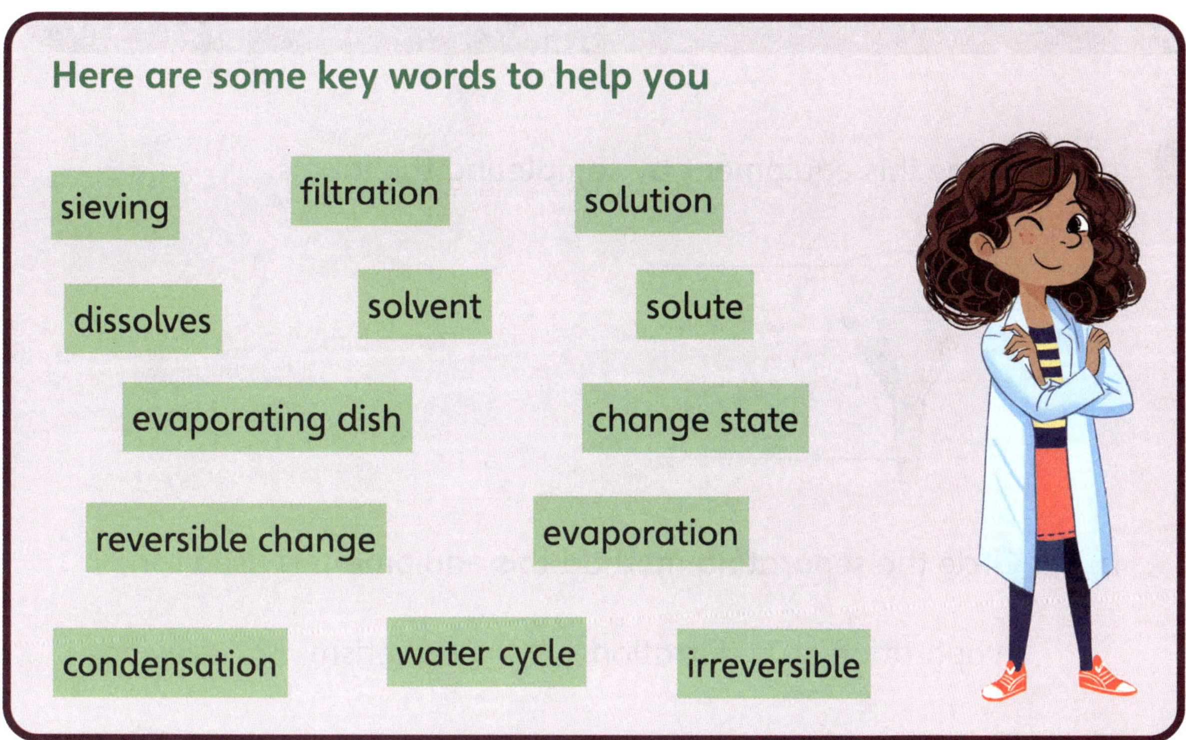

Choose two key words from the box above.
Write or draw what they mean.

Sieving or filtration?

1 a) Name this equipment by completing the labels.

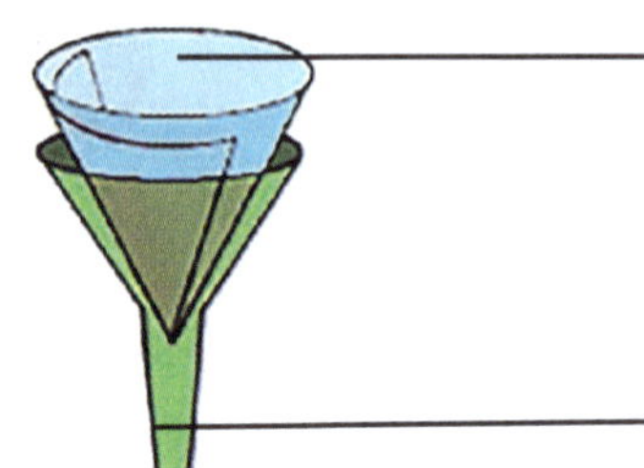

b) Circle the separating method this equipment is used for.

evaporation   filtration   magnetism   sieving

2 a) Name this piece of equipment.

____

b) Circle the separating method it is used for.

evaporation   filtration   magnetism   sieving

3 Which separating method should you use to separate:

a) a mixture of grains of different sizes?

____

b) a solid and a liquid where the solid has **not** dissolved?

____

4 A learner uses this equipment to separate a mixture of sand and water.

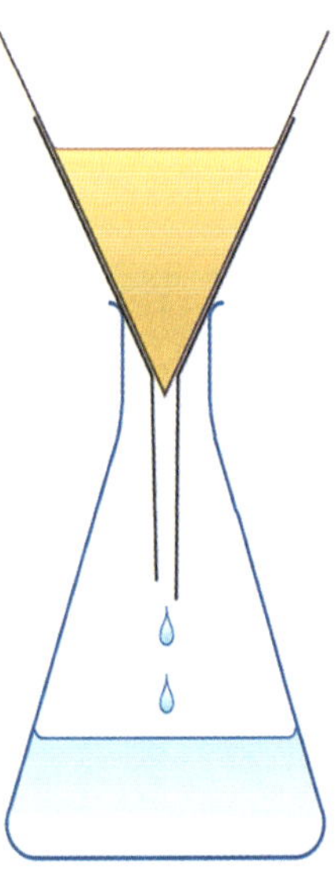

a) Label **sand** and **water** on this diagram.

b) This diagram shows the same mixture magnified.

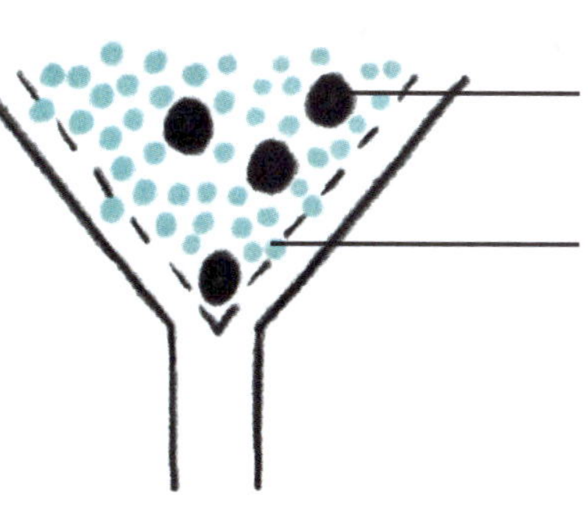

Label **sand** and **water** on this diagram.

5 Complete the table by putting **one** tick (✓) in each row to show the best method of separating these mixtures.

Mixture	Sieving?	Filtration?
sand and water		
raisins and flour		
dried pasta and sugar		
soil and water		
rocks and soil		

6 A learner has a mixture of nuts and flour to separate.

She has sieves with different mesh sizes. She cannot decide which sieve to use.

Explain to her how to choose which sieve to use. Include a drawing to help you explain.

____

____

____

____

____

____

Solutions

1 a) Name these two pieces of equipment.

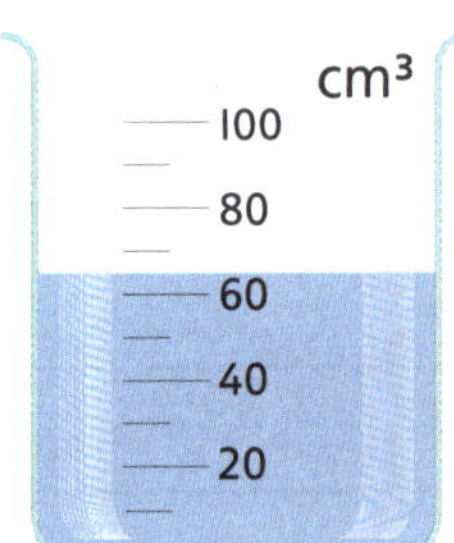

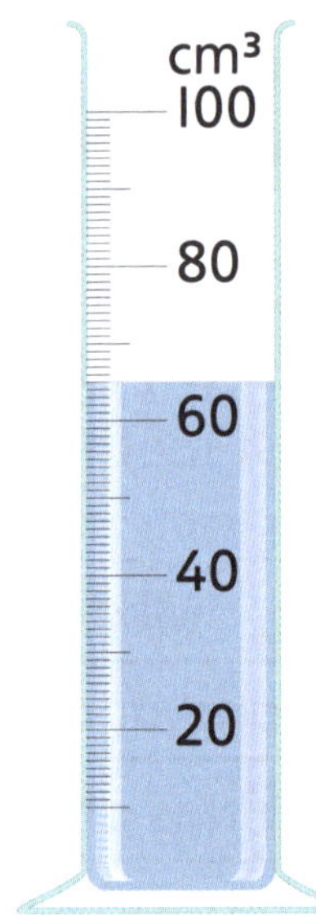

_______________________   _______________________

b) They both contain the same volume of water.

(i) How much water does each contain? _____________ cm³

(ii) In which piece of equipment can this volume be measured more accurately? Explain why.

____

____

____

2 A learner has a mixture of sand, salt and water.

a) Circle the solute from the list below.

salt   salt solution   sand   water

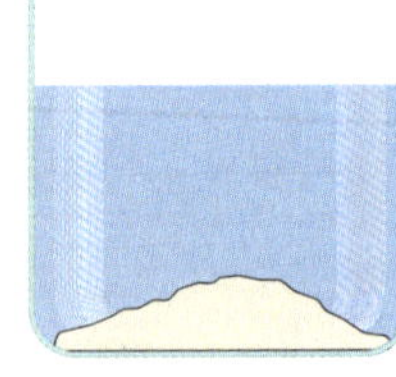

b) Circle the solvent.

salt   salt solution   sand   water

c) Circle the solution.

salt and sand   sand and water

salt and water   water only

3 A learner puts some blue crystals of copper sulfate into some water.
   He stirs the blue liquid until it looks clear.

copper sulfate   **copper sulfate in water**

a) Write **one** word to describe what has happened to the
   copper sulfate.

   The copper sulfate has _____________________ in the water.

b) Why did the learner stir the liquid?

   ____

c) Write the scientific word for each substance in the table.

   All the words start with letter 's'.

Substance	Scientific word
copper sulfate	
water	
copper sulfate and water together	

Finding the dissolved solute

1 A learner puts some salt into some water.

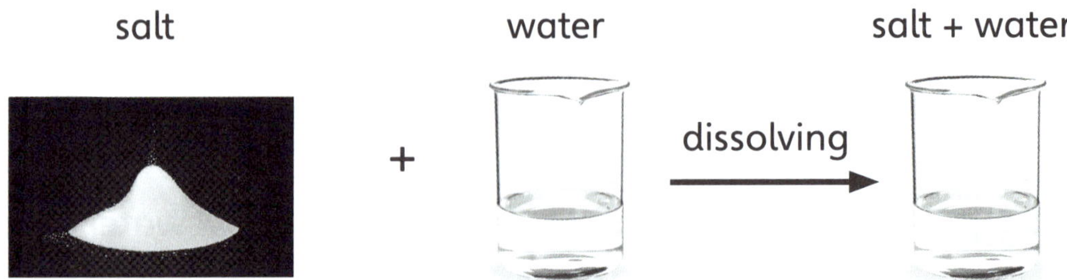

a)   Name the equipment the water is in.

____

b)   Write **two** different ways that he could make the salt dissolve faster.

1. ____

2. ____

c)   Write the scientific word for each substance in the table.

All the words start with letter 's'.

Substance	Scientific word
water	
salt	
salt and water together	

2 Another learner has some rock salt. She wants to separate the salt from the rocks and sand.

Describe what she is doing next to each picture.

States of matter

1 a) (i) Circle the solids.

   (ii) Write 'L' next to the liquids.

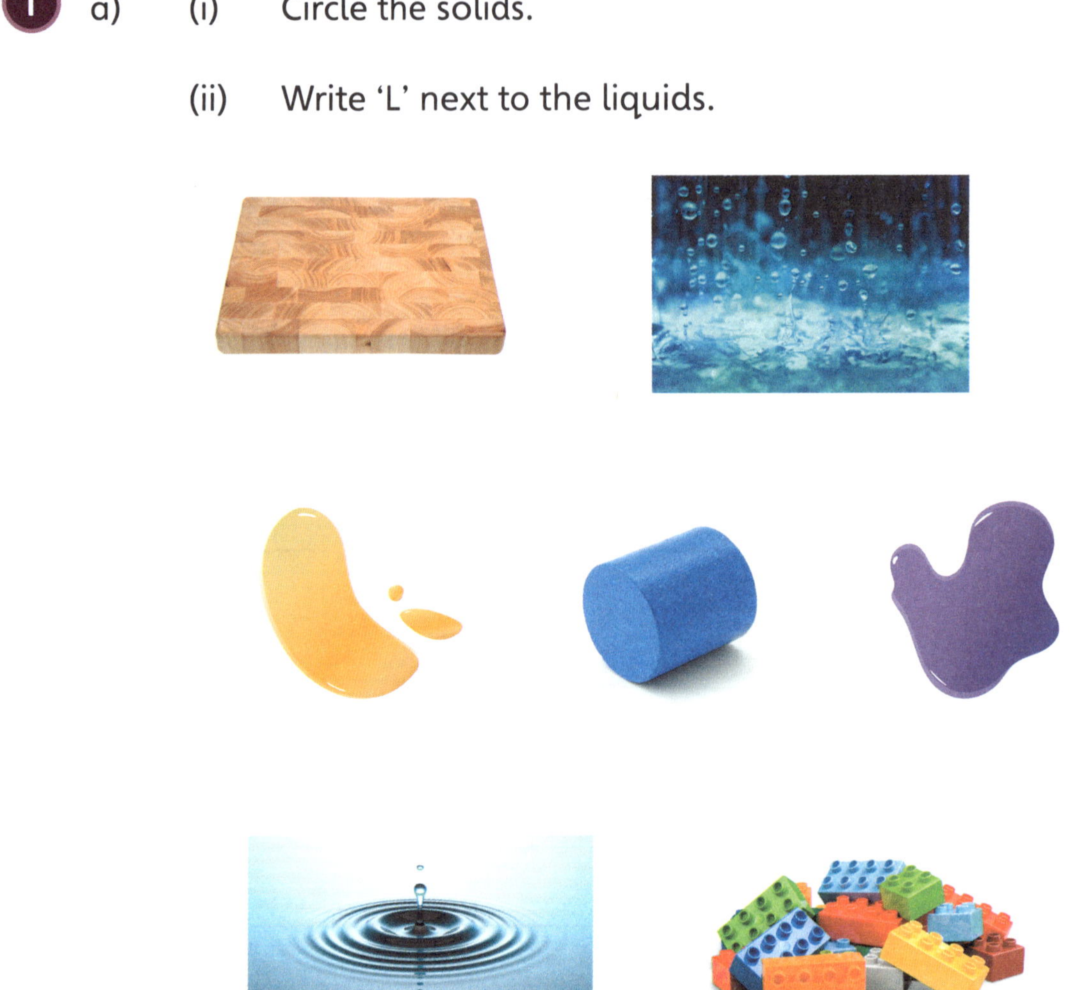

b) Write **one** other state of matter not shown in the pictures.

2 a) What property of a liquid does this picture show?

b) What property of a solid does this picture show?

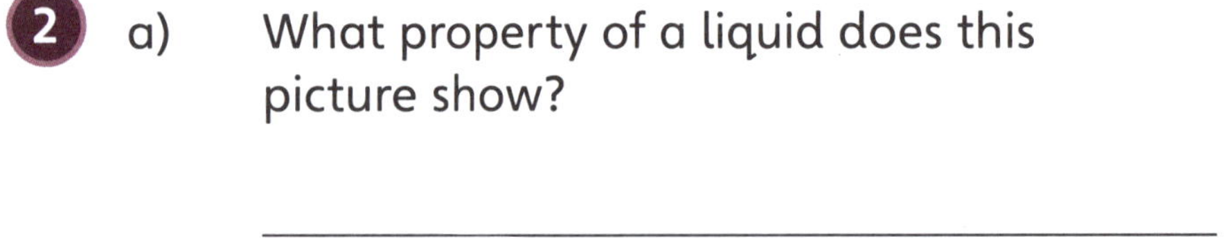

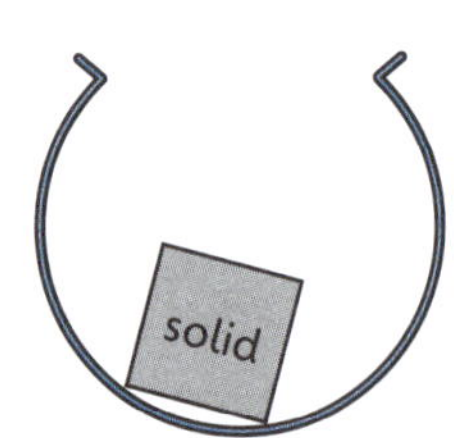

c)   What property of a solid does this picture show?

____

____

d)   What property of a gas does this picture show?

____

____

3   Imagine you are explaining to someone what solids, liquids and gases are like. Write some of their properties under each heading.

Solids

____

____

____

Liquids

____

____

____

Gases

____

____

____

Changes of state

1. a) What is happening to this ice lolly?

   ____

   b) Suggest why this is happening.

   ____

2. The picture shows someone pouring water to make ice cubes.

   a) Circle the state of the water in the jug.

   solid   liquid   gas

   b) Here is one of the ice cubes. Circle its state.

   solid   liquid   gas

   c) Name the change of state that has taken place.

   ____

   d) The ice cube is left in a warm place. What change of state happens?

   ____

3. Someone is heating water in a pan.

   a) Circle the state of the water in the pan.

   solid   liquid   gas

   b) The water level in the pan goes down. What has happened to the water?

   ____

c) A window near the pan now looks like this.

Explain why the window has drops of water on it.

____

____

____

4 A learner draws this diagram to show changes of state.

a) Write the name of **one** change of state in the box beside each arrow.

b) (i)   Circle the **two** arrows that show heating.

(ii) What do the other arrows show?

____

The water cycle

1 The picture shows the water cycle.

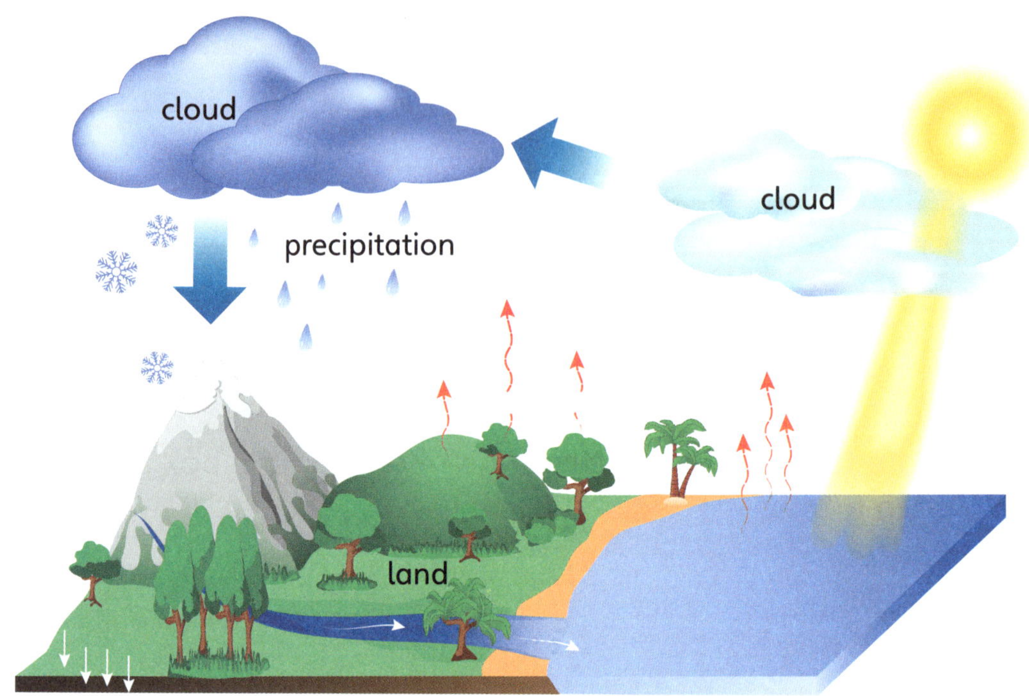

a)   Write **Sun** and **sea** in the correct places on the diagram.

b)   Give **two** examples to show what *precipitation* means.

1. _________________________   2. _________________________

c)   (i)   Which change of state is shown by these arrows?
            Write it above them on the big picture.

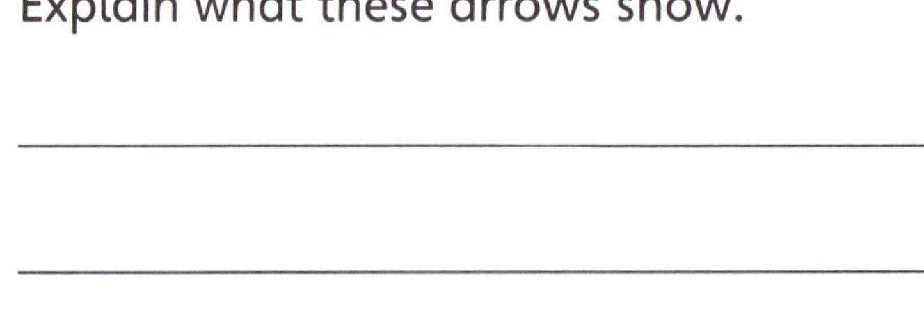

     (ii) What is heating the sea water to make it
            change state?

            ____

d)   Explain what these arrows show.

____

____

e)   Write the word **condensation** in the correct place on the big picture on the opposite page.

f)   Explain how these clouds are formed. There are words in the box to help you write your explanation.

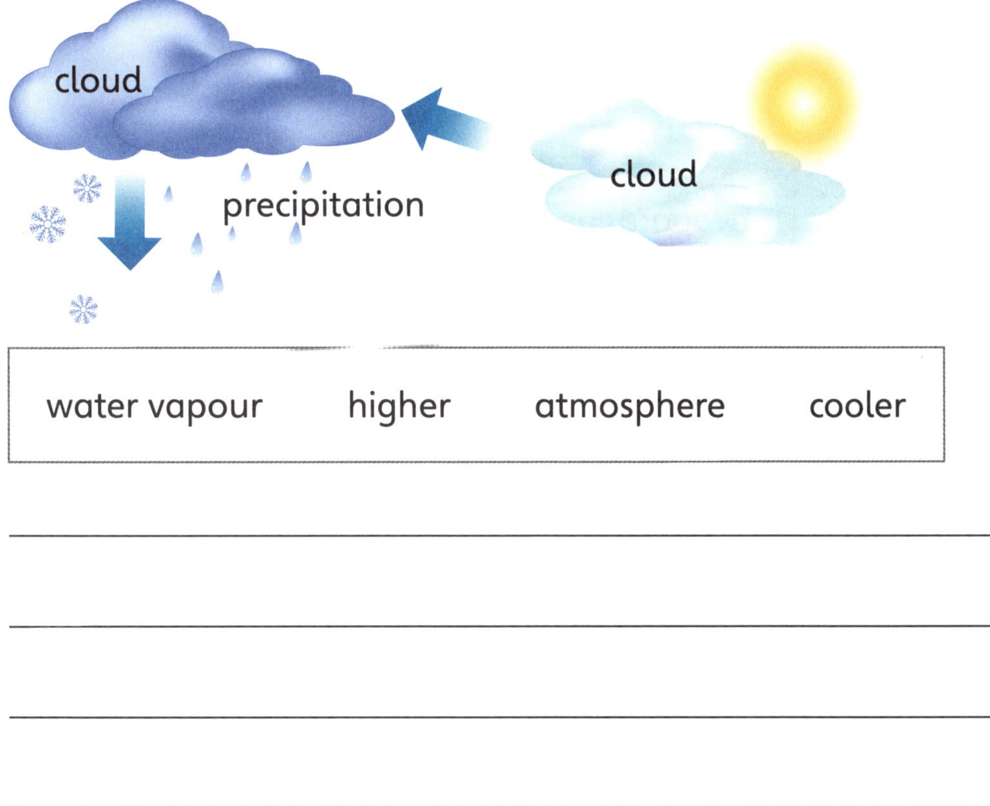

____

____

____

____

2   Complete the sentence about the water cycle.

The water cycle is the path that all the _________________ on Earth

follows as it changes from one _________________ to another.

3   Evaporation and condensation are reversible changes.

Explain what *reversible change* means.

____

____

Irreversible changes

1 a)   Circle the irreversible change.

b)   What kind of change is shown in the other three pictures?

____

2   The picture shows some bread dough.

a)   Draw what it will look like after it is cooked.

b)   What sort of change is this? ___________________________

3   Name the new material that has formed here.

____

4   The picture shows some logs.

   a)   Draw what they will look like after they are burnt.

burning

   b)   When the logs burn, smoke is made.
        How does this show that burning is an **irreversible** change?

   ____

   ____

5   These eggs are cooking.
        Explain why this is an **irreversible** change.

   ____

   ____

6   A learner dissolves some salt in a beaker of water.

   Is dissolving an **irreversible** change?

   Tick (✓) **one** box and give a reason for your choice.

   Yes   ☐   No   ☐

   Reason ____

   ____

Investigating irreversible changes

1   a)   Name the **irreversible** change shown in the picture.

          Write it above the arrow.

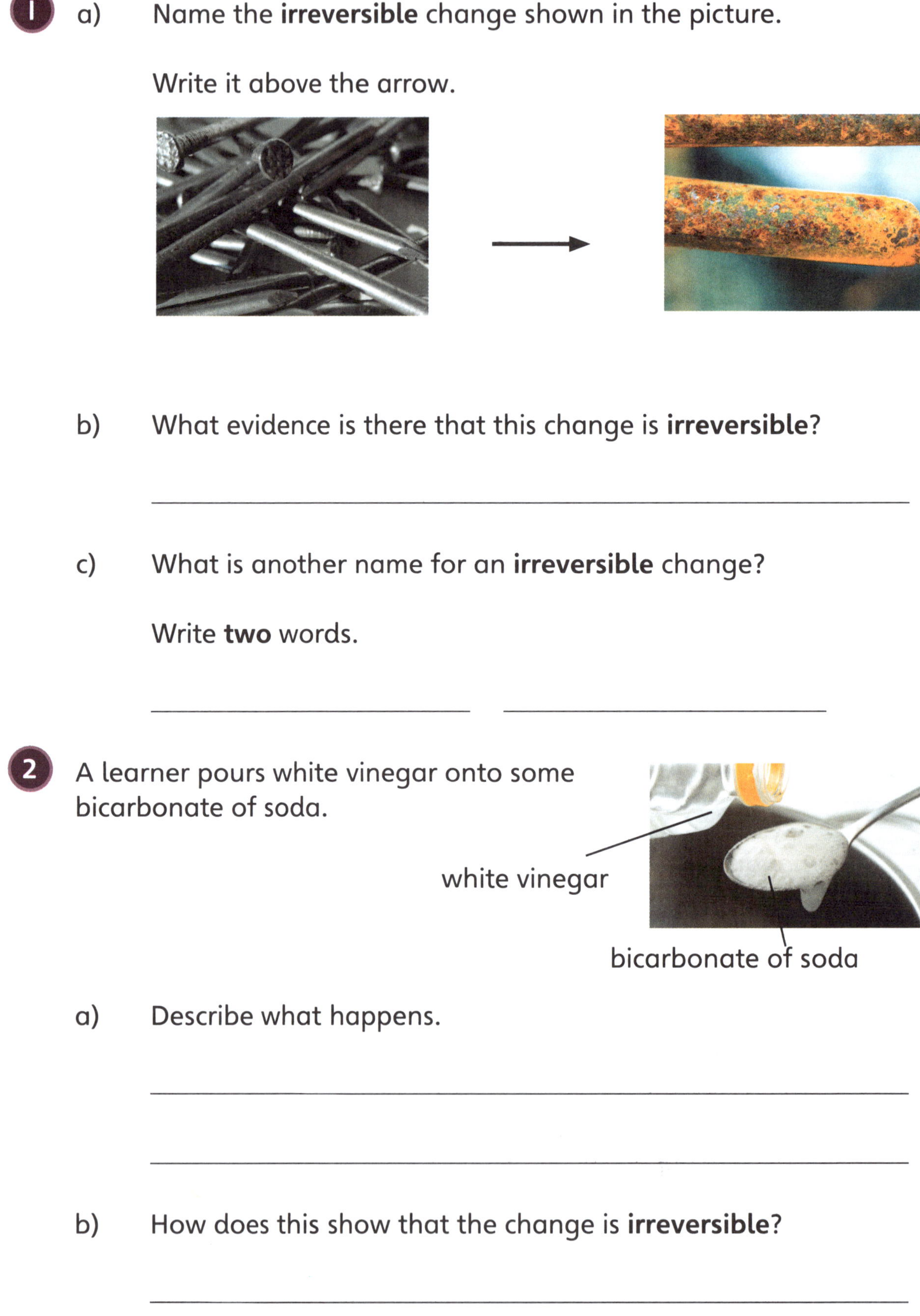

     b)   What evidence is there that this change is **irreversible**?

____

     c)   What is another name for an **irreversible** change?

          Write **two** words.

______________________   ______________________

2   A learner pours white vinegar onto some bicarbonate of soda.

     a)   Describe what happens.

____

____

     b)   How does this show that the change is **irreversible**?

____

3

a) Which of these is an **irreversible** change? Circle **one** word.

burning   dissolving   freezing   mixing

b) Each picture shows an **irreversible** change.

Describe the evidence you can see in each picture that shows new materials have formed.

Irreversible change	Evidence that new materials have formed
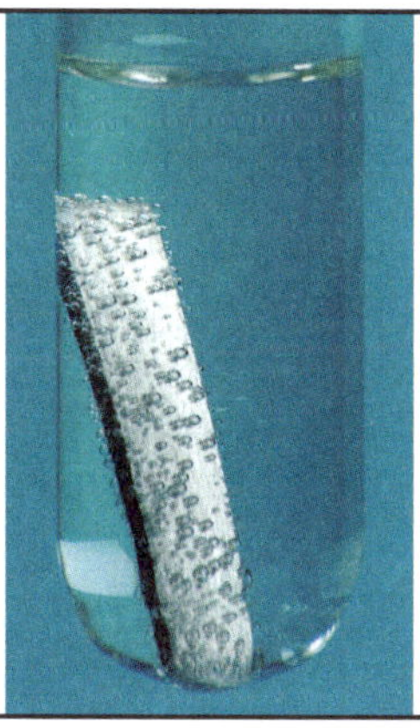	______________________ ______________________ ______________________
	______________________ ______________________ ______________________
	______________________ ______________________ ______________________

More carbon dioxide

Try the investigations in your textbook.

1 Use carbon dioxide to inflate a balloon.

a) What equipment do you need?

____

____

b) Explain what you did in your own words. Number the steps to make it easier to explain.

____

____

____

____

____

c) Draw and label a diagram of what happened.

Try to draw it like a scientific diagram.

d) Write **one** improvement you could make if you did this again.

____

____

2 Make a volcano.

a) What equipment do you need?

____

____

____

b) Draw your volcano or stick in a picture of it. Label it.

c) How can you make your volcano erupt better or for longer?

____

____

____

____

____

d) Write **one** improvement you could make if you did this again.

____

____

Comparing reversible and irreversible changes

1 Complete the sentences about reversible and irreversible changes. Use each word from the box **once** only.

chemical   mixing   new   materials   physical   state   gas   colour

Reversible changes are ________________ changes.

No new ________________ are formed.

Changes of ________________ are reversible changes.

Dissolving and ________________ are also reversible changes.

Irreversible changes are ________________ changes.

One or more ________________ materials are formed.

We can see evidence of irreversible changes by looking for changes in temperature or a ________________ change.

Sometimes, bubbles of ________________ are made.

2 The diagram shows dissolving, which is a **reversible** change.

Explain how to get the dissolved salt back.

____

____

____

3 The diagram shows a mixture of sand and water. 

   a)   Write **one** word that describes substances such as sand that do not dissolve.

   ____

   b)   Name a method you could use to separate the sand from the water.

   ____

4 Candles are made of wax, which is a solid.

When the candle is lit, some wax changes to a liquid and flows down the sides of the candle. Some of the wax burns.

   a)   (i)   What happens to the liquid wax as it cools?

   ____

        (ii)   What sort of change is this?   _____________________

   b)   (i)   What happens to the candle as the wax burns?

   ____

        (ii)   What sort of change is this?   _____________________

        (iii)   What do the arrows on the picture show?

   ____

What have I learned?

1 I can explain, with examples, that mixtures can be separated using a sieve or filter.

I know this because I can write one mixture that can be separated by each method.

sieving: ____

filtration: ____

2 I understand the terms *dissolving*, *solution*, *solvent* and *solute*. I can explain how a solute can be recovered from a solution.

I know this because I can label the diagram with these four words.

I also know that I can get the solute back from the solution by

_______________________________ the solvent.

3 I understand that melting, freezing, evaporation and condensation are changes of state. I can also explain that changes of state require changes of temperature.

I know this because I can write **melting**, **freezing**, **evaporation** or **condensation** above each arrow. I can write **heating** or **cooling** below each arrow.

solid ⟶ liquid ⟶ gas

gas ⟶ liquid ⟶ solid

4 I can describe the role of **evaporation** and **condensation** in the water cycle.

I know this because I can write both words on this diagram.

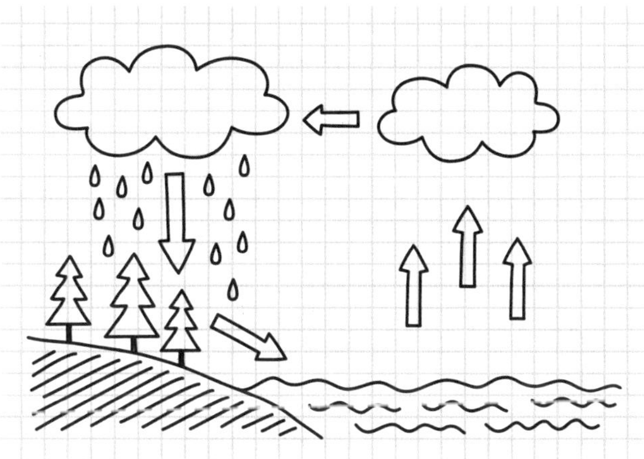

5 I understand that dissolving, mixing and changes of state are **reversible** changes.

I know this by looking at my answers to questions 1, 2 and 3.

6 I can describe simple **irreversible** changes, for example the ones that happen when vinegar (an acid) and bicarbonate of soda are mixed. I can also explain that these changes result in the formation of new materials.

I know this because I can write **three irreversible** changes that might happen in a reaction.

1. ____

2. _______________________   _______________________

3. ____

I also know this because I can list **two** observations that show new materials are being formed.

1. ____

2. ____

Forces in air and water

Forces make things move. If you drop your pencil, it falls to the floor. This is because the force of gravity pulls falling objects towards the centre of Earth. Friction is an invisible contact force that slows moving objects. Objects moving through air or through water are slowed by forces too.

In this topic we will learn:

- that unsupported objects fall towards the Earth because of the force of gravity acting between the Earth and the falling object

- that weight is a force and forces are measured in newtons (N)

- that more than one force can act on an object at the same time

- that friction can be used to improve how well an object grips a surface

- that friction acts on moving objects to slow them down

- that friction can act between solid surfaces and air and water

- that air resistance and water resistance are forces that reduce the speed at which objects move

- about the effects of these three forces acting between moving surfaces

- about how the shape of objects can be used to reduce the effects of water and air resistance, including the term *streamlined*.

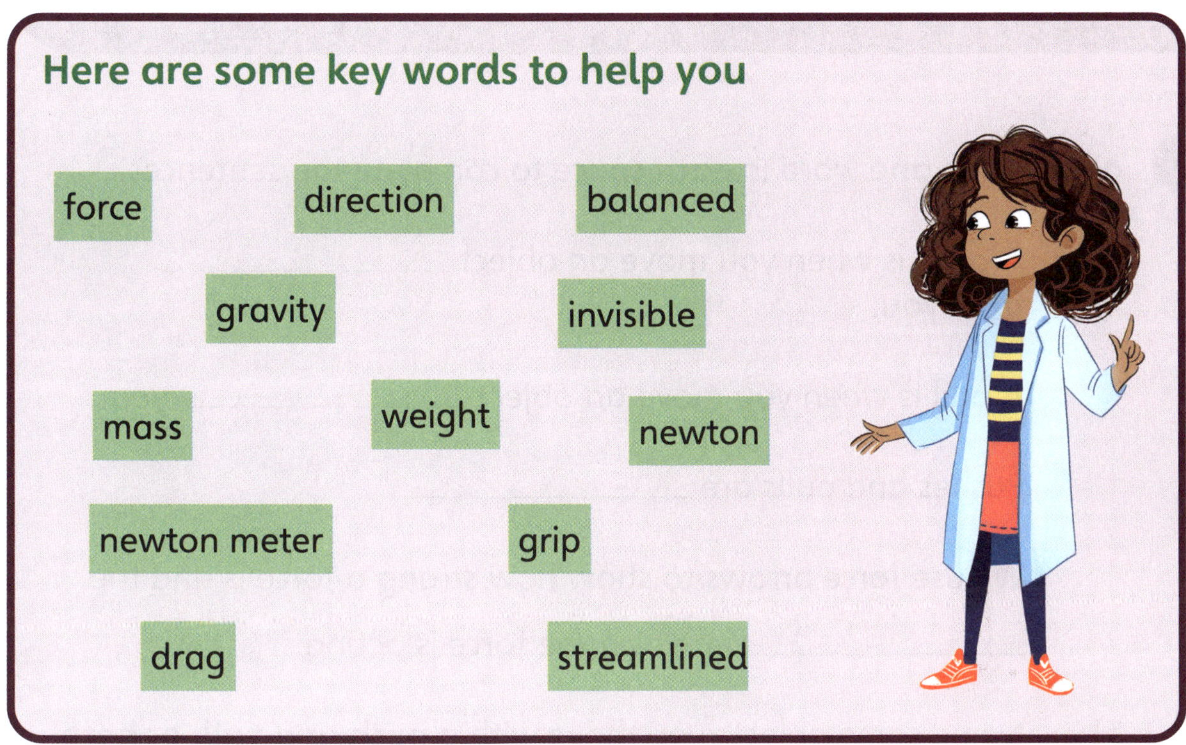

Choose two key words from the box above.
Write or draw what they mean.

1 a) Write **one** word in each space to complete the sentences.

A push is when you move an object ____________________ from you.

A pull is when you move an object ____________________ you.

Pushes and pulls are ____________________ .

We use force arrows to show how strong a force is and the ____________________ in which the force is acting.

b) Name some objects you move with a **push** or a **pull**, or **both**.

push	pull	both

2 a) Explain why this box does not move.

____

____

b) Suggest **two** ways the children could change what they are doing that will make the box move.

1. ______________________________________

2. ______________________________________

3 In this game, the red tie in the middle of a rope is above a stone.

To win, one team must pull the rope with enough force to make the tie move to their side of the stone.

Picture 1

a) In **Picture 1**, no one is winning.

    (i) What does this tell you about the force with which each team is pulling?

    ____

    (ii) Draw **two** force arrows on **Picture 1** to show the pulling forces.

Picture 2

b) (i) Draw **two** force arrows on **Picture 2**.

    (ii) Explain what is happening in **Picture 2**.

    ____

    ____

    ____

Gravity

1 a)   Draw an apple falling from this tree.

b)   Name the force that acts on the falling apple.

____

c)   Draw **four** apple trees in different places around this picture of Earth.

Show **one** apple falling from each tree.

2   a)   Gravity is a *non-contact force*. What does this mean?

____

____

    b)   Name another non-contact force. _______________________

3   Complete the sentences about gravity.

Gravity is an invisible force that _________________ everything down

towards the _________________ of the _________________.

The force of gravity is weaker on the _________________ than
on Earth.

Gravitational forces keep all the planets in _________________

around the _________________.

Gravitational forces keep the Moon in _________________ around
Earth too.

4   This learner jumps into the air.

    a)   Why does she come back down again?

____

____

    b)   If Earth did not have gravity, predict what would happen when
         the learner jumps.

____

____

1 a) Name this piece of equipment.

____

b) Complete the sentences about mass.

All objects are made of _______________________.

The amount of matter in an object is called its _______________.

The more matter in an object, the _______________________ its mass.

We measure mass in _______________________ (g) and _______________________ (kg).

2 a) Name this piece of equipment.

____

b) Complete the sentences about weight.

Weight is a _______________________.

Weight is the force with which _______________. acts on an object.

We measure forces in _______________ (N).

c)   Write the weight that each piece of equipment shows.

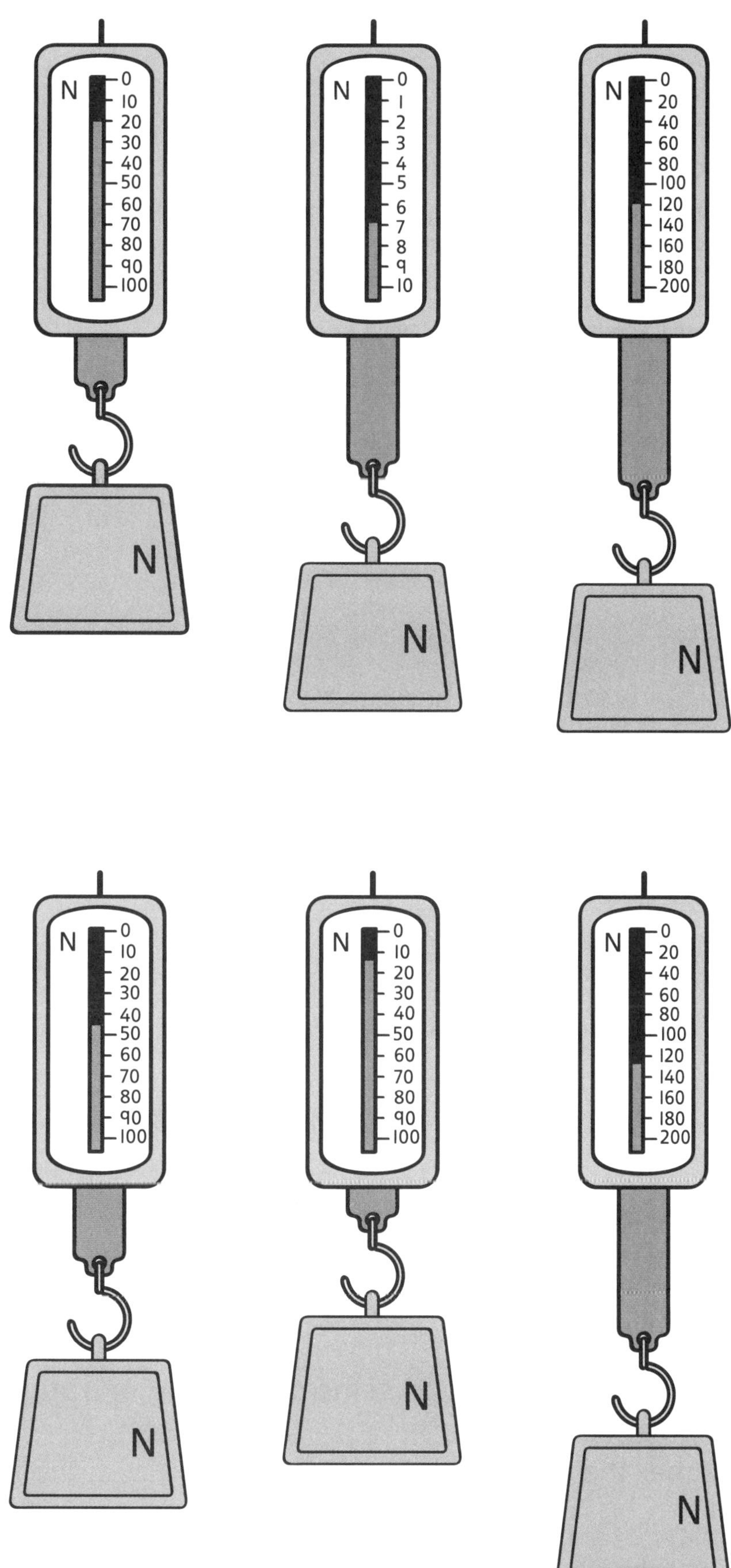

Friction

1 Circle the **two** words or phrases that describe friction.

a contact force   absorbent   a non-contact force

invisible   rough   transparent

2 This car is moving along a road.

a)   Circle **two** places where friction is acting between solid surfaces.

b)   What does friction do to the car's movement?

____

3 Write **more friction** or **less friction** above the correct toy car and complete the sentence underneath.

_______________________________   _______________________________

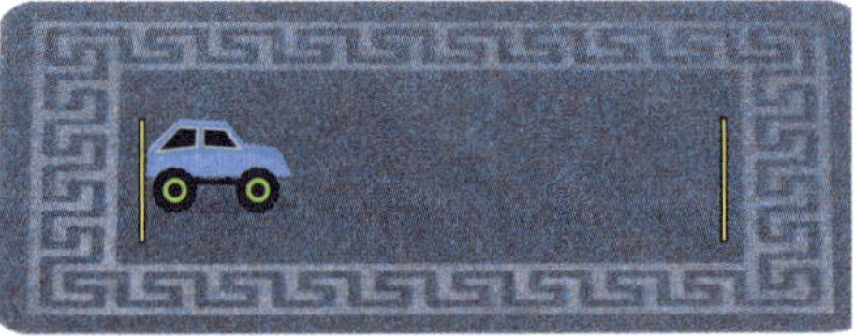

car moving on **smooth** floor same car moving on **rough** floor

The rougher the surface, the _____________________ the friction force.

4 The forces acting on this box are balanced.

The box is not moving.

a) How do the force arrows show that the forces acting on the box are balanced?

____

b) How can this person make the box move?

____

5 a) This boat is moving through water.

    (i) Name one force that is slowing the boat.

    ____

    (ii) Draw an arrow on the picture to show the direction in which this slowing force acts on the boat.

b) This aeroplane is moving through the air.

    (i) Name the force that is slowing the aeroplane.

    ____

    (ii) Draw an arrow on the picture to show the direction in which this slowing force acts on the aeroplane.

Investigating grip

1 Circle the shoe that has most grip.

2 Describe each picture using the word **grip** in **all four** answers.

 **tyre chains**	__________________________ __________________________ __________________________
 **diving board**	__________________________ __________________________ __________________________
 **walking in mud**	__________________________ __________________________ __________________________
 **steps**	__________________________ __________________________ __________________________ __________________________

3 Investigate the force that is needed to make different shoes just start to move.

a) What will you change?

____

b) What will you measure? _______________________________

c) Write **two** things that you will keep the same each time.

1. ____

2. ____

d) Why should you repeat your measurements for each shoe?

____

e) Draw a results table and write your results in it.

f) Write a conclusion.

____

____

____

Reducing frictional forces

1 The picture shows some forces acting on a moving car.

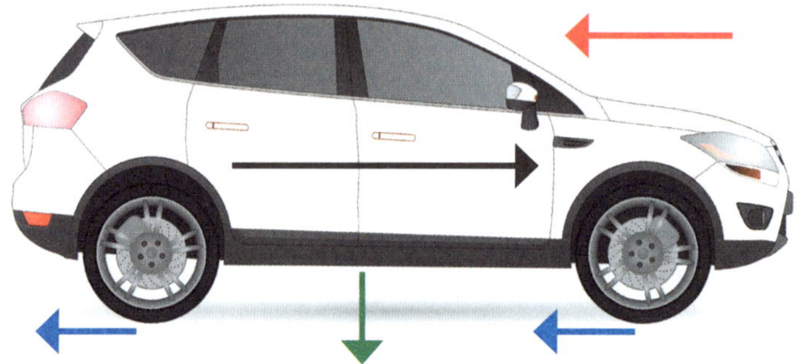

a) Name each force. One has been done for you.

b) Which force is caused by gravity pulling on the car?

____

c) Circle all the arrows that show forces slowing the car down.

2 The pictures show the shape of two cars.

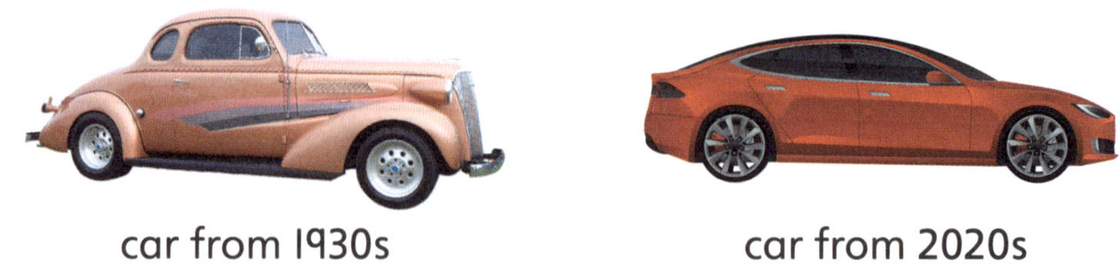

a) Complete the sentence with **one** word to compare their shapes.

The **2020s** car is more ____________________________.

b) How does this difference in shape help the 2020s car when it moves?

____

____

3 Do some research for yourself about a sport where reducing friction is important. There are some ideas in your textbook.

Include a drawing, or stick in a picture, as well as using words.

Investigating streamlining

1 Investigate how fast different shapes move through liquid.

    a)   Write your scientific question.

    b)   What will you change?

    c)   Describe what you will measure.

    d)   (i)   How much modelling clay will you use to keep each shape the same mass?

           (ii)   Draw the shapes you will use in the space below.

    e)   Write **two** ways to make this a **fair** comparison.

        1.

        2.

2 Draw and label your equipment with one of the shapes inside it.

3 a) Draw the **fastest** shape and the **slowest** shape.

fastest	slowest

b) Suggest why these two shapes moved at different speeds.

____

____

4 Suggest **one** improvement to your investigation.

____

____

What have I learned?

1. I can explain that unsupported objects fall towards the Earth because of the force of gravity acting between the Earth and the falling object.

I know this because I can draw a force arrow to show the direction in which gravity acts on a falling apple.

2. I understand that weight is a force and forces are measured in newtons (N).

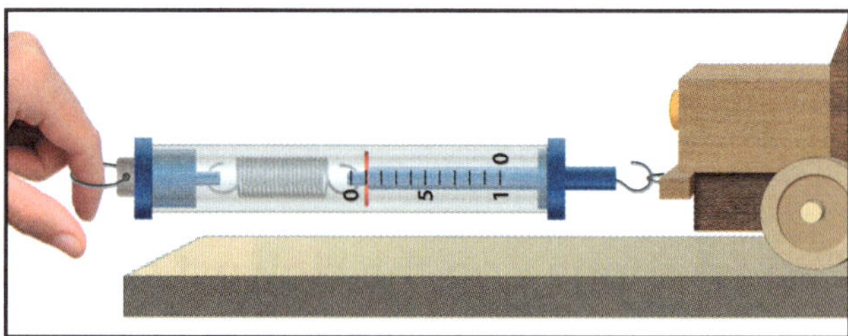

I know this because I can read this force meter. ________________

3. I understand that more than one force can act on an object at the same time.

I know this because I can draw force arrows to show weight and air resistance on this moving car.

4. I understand how friction can be used to improve how well an object grips a surface.

I know this because I can write **two** ways that we use grip to stop us from slipping.

1. ____

2. ____

5 I know that friction acts on moving objects to slow them down.

I understand that friction can act between solid surfaces and air and water.

I know this because I can show where friction acts to slow this moving car.

6 I understand that air resistance and water resistance are forces that reduce the speed at which objects move.

I can also identify the effects of forces acting between moving surfaces.

I know this because I can draw force arrows to show how air resistance and water resistance act on these objects.

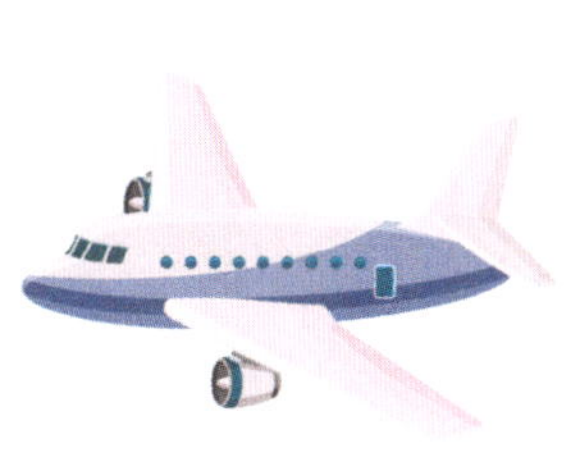

7 I can describe how the shape of objects can be used to reduce the effects of water and air resistance, including the term *streamlined*.

I know this because I can draw a shape that moves quickly through wallpaper paste and one that moves more slowly.

quickly	slowly

Electricity: changing circuits

Electrical circuits are not always simple. Imagine how many wires are connected to make the electrical circuits in a house, office or school. Drawing circuits using symbols makes them easier for everyone to understand.

In this topic we will learn:

- about the need for universally recognised symbols for electrical components

- how to draw and identify recognised electrical component symbols for a bulb, buzzer, battery, cell, wire, switch and motor

- to use and interpret recognised symbols for components when drawing or designing simple series circuits

- to link the brightness of a bulb or the volume of a buzzer with the number and voltage of cells used in the circuit

- to compare and give reasons for variations in how components function.

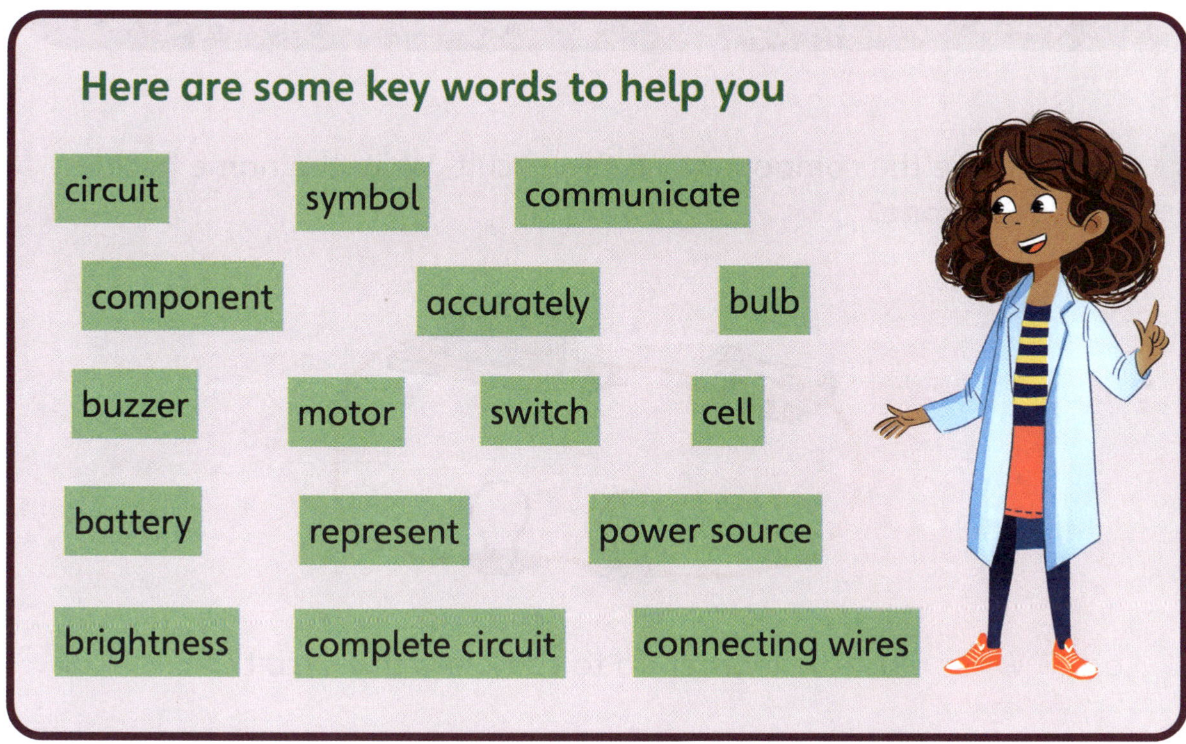

Choose two key words from the box above.
Write or draw what they mean.

Universal symbols

1 a) Name the components in this circuit. Write the name beside each one.

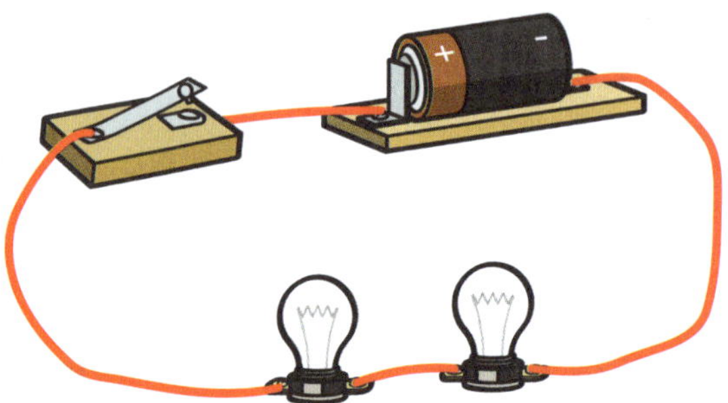

  b) What must the learner do to complete this circuit?

  ____

2 Symbols help us to communicate, whatever language we speak. Look at the symbols on these road signs.

  a) Would you go along this road?
      What do you think the symbols mean?

  ____

  ____

  b) Suggest what you **cannot** do on this road.

  ____

  ____

3 You met these components in Year 4. Name them.

a)

____

b)

____

c) Draw a labelled scientific diagram for this equipment.

picture   **diagram**

d) Draw the symbol for this component.

picture   **symbol**

4 Complete the sentence.

Scientists use the same set of _____________________ for electrical

_____________________ so that everyone can understand them,

whatever _____________________ they speak.

Circuit symbols

1 Complete the table with the name and symbol of each component.

Component	Name of component	Symbol

2 a) Explain the difference between a **cell** and a **battery**, using these pictures to help.

____

____

b) Which part of the symbol for a cell represents which end?

Write **+** or **–** above each line of the symbol below.

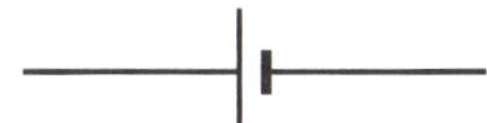

c) Explain why the bulb in this circuit does **not** light.

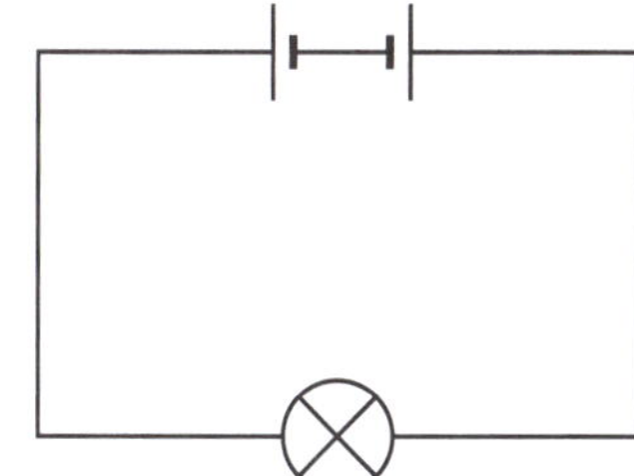

____

3 Draw a circuit diagram showing **a cell**, **two bulbs** and an **open switch** connected with **wires**.

Making circuits

1 Name these components and draw their symbol. One has been done for you.

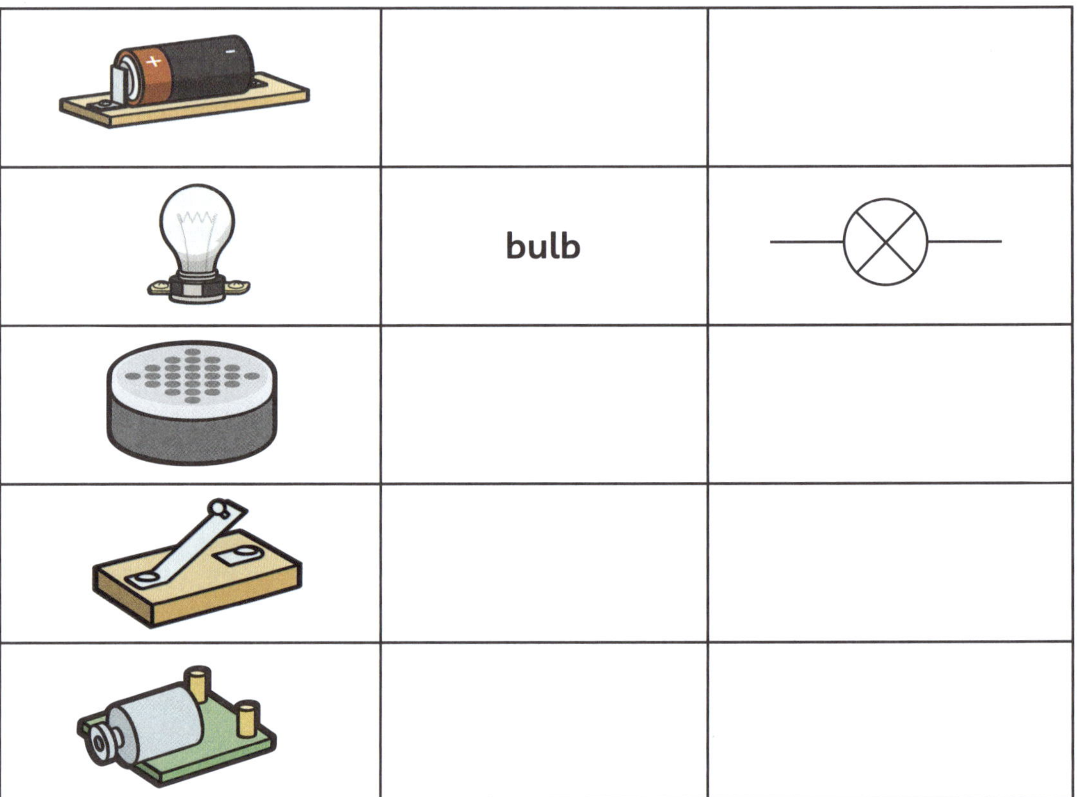

	bulb	

2 Draw a circuit diagram for each of these circuits.

a)

b)

c)

d)

Investigating how components function

1   Describe the brightness of each bulb by writing underneath it.

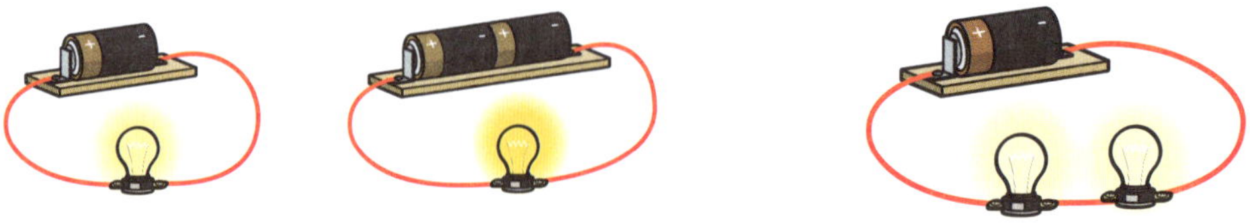

Write **one** conclusion using at least one word ending in -er.

Conclusion: ____

____

____

2   Describe ways to make the buzzer **louder** or **quieter**.

You may have more than one idea for each.

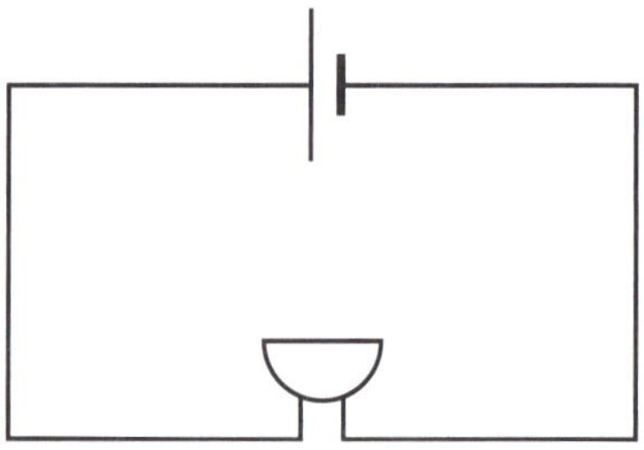

Louder: _______________________________________

____

____

Quieter: _______________________________________

____

____

Write **one** conclusion using at least one word ending in -er.

Conclusion: ____

____

____

3 Describe ways to make the motor turn **faster** or **slower**.

You may have more than one idea for each.

Faster: _______________________________

____

____

Slower: _______________________________

____

____

Write **one** conclusion using at least one word ending in -er.

Conclusion: ____________________________

____

____

4 a) What is the function of a **switch** and a **cell** in a circuit?

Switch: ________________________________

Cell: __________________________________

b) Describe what the wires of a circuit are made of and why these materials are used.

Inside: ________________________________

____

Outside: _______________________________

____

Make a windmill

Try to make a model similar to the windmill shown in your textbook.

Design one, even if you cannot make it.

1 Draw the circuit for your model.

2 Draw your finished model or take a photograph of it and stick it in.

3 Describe how you made your model and any improvements you could make.

____

____

____

____

____

____

____

____

____

4 Design a different model using a **buzzer**, a **motor** or **both**.

What have I learned?

1 I understand the need for universally recognised symbols for electrical components.

I know this because I can write a reason why we use these symbols.

____

____

2 I can draw and identify recognised electrical component symbols for a **bulb**, **buzzer**, **battery**, **cell**, **wire**, **switch** and **motor**.

I know this because I can draw them here:

bulb	buzzer	battery	cell

wire	switch	motor

3 I can use and interpret recognised symbols for components when drawing or designing simple series circuits.

I know this because I can draw a circuit diagram for this circuit.

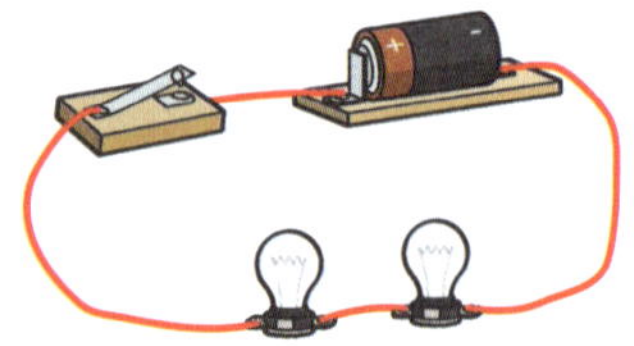

4 a)　I can link the brightness of a bulb or the volume of a buzzer with the number and voltage of cells used in the circuit.

b)　I can also compare and give reasons for variations in how components function. This includes:

- the brightness of bulbs

- the loudness of buzzers

- the on/off position of switches and

- the speed of motors.

I know this because I can label these bulbs as **dim**, **bright** or **very bright**.

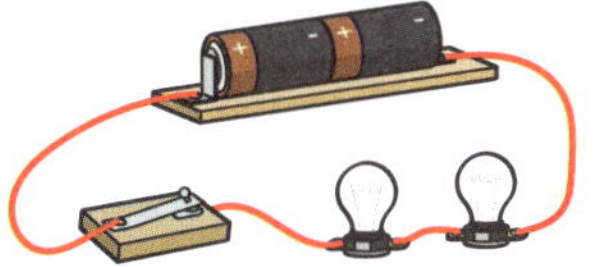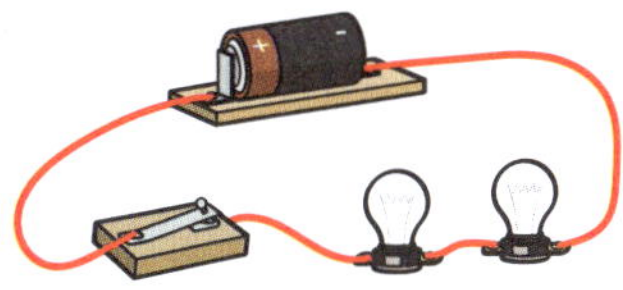

_______________　_______________　_______________

I also know this because I can complete these sentences.

The more cells, the _____________________ a motor turns because there is a higher voltage.

The more cells, the _____________________ a buzzer sounds because there is a higher voltage.

I also know this because I can describe the function of a switch in a circuit.

____

Revision

Think about when you first started learning science and there were lots of new words with precise meanings. Now you know them, or you can go back and learn them! This revision section summarises all the topics that are tested in the end of Year 6 examination.

In this topic we will learn:

- the key points for the topics tested in the end of Year 6 examination

- the key points for investigating science

- that command words in tests and examinations are words that tell us what to do

- about the units needed for measurements in science.

It means that you read some of your notes, then cover them up and try to remember them. Then look to see if you remembered everything correctly.

Or listen to your recording, repeat the key points, then listen again to check.

Make sure you take regular breaks and drink water to stay hydrated. That all helps too.

You can do 'look, cover, say' with vocabulary too. Use pieces of paper or cards. Write one word on the front and its meaning on the back. Do that as you work on each topic.

That's a good idea! Then you can look at the word and try to remember its meaning.

Another day you can look at the meanings and try to remember the correct word. Classmates or people at home can test you too.

Revision: Feeding relationships

1 a) Draw the **two** missing arrows in this food chain.

grass   rabbit   fox

b) Which is the producer?

____

c) Which is a carnivore?

____

2 Write the correct word beside each definition.

	a living thing in a food chain that can make its own food
	an animal that hunts other animals to eat
	an animal that is hunted by other animals
	an animal in a food chain that eats other living things
	an animal that eats other animals
	an animal that eats plants

3 This is a food web in a pond.

dragonfly larva

common frog

heron

stickleback

microscopic animals

mayfly larva

pond snail

microscopic algae

pondweed

a) Name **two** producers.

   1. _______________________   2. _______________________

b) Name **one** predator of the stickleback. _______________________

c) Name **two** consumers.

   1. _______________________   2. _______________________

d) Name **one** of the common frog's prey _______________________

e) Draw **one** food chain that includes the pond snail. *Draw* a food chain means use words and arrows, not pictures.

f) Predict what might happen to the number of common frogs if the number of herons increases a lot. Give **one** reason.

____

____

Revision: Variation and classification

1 a) Name the **five vertebrate** groups.

I. _________________________   2. _________________________

3. _________________________   4. _________________________

5. _________________________

b) Name **four** of the many **invertebrate** groups.

I. _________________________   2. _________________________

3. _________________________   4. _________________________

c) Write **one** important difference between vertebrates and invertebrates.

____

____

2 Put **one** tick (✓) in each row to show whether the named plants are **flowering** or **non-flowering** plants.

	Flowering plants	Non-flowering plants
ferns		
mosses		
buttercups		
grasses		

3 a) Identify this animal. _________________________

b) What is its habitat?

____

c) Is it a vertebrate or an invertebrate? ___________________

d) Describe its body. ___________________

____

4 a) Draw and colour a buttercup flower.

b) Describe this buttercup leaf. ___________________

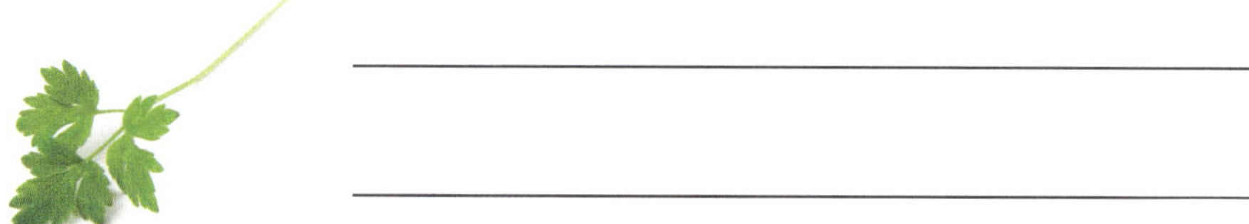

____

____

5 Use the key to identify these flowers.

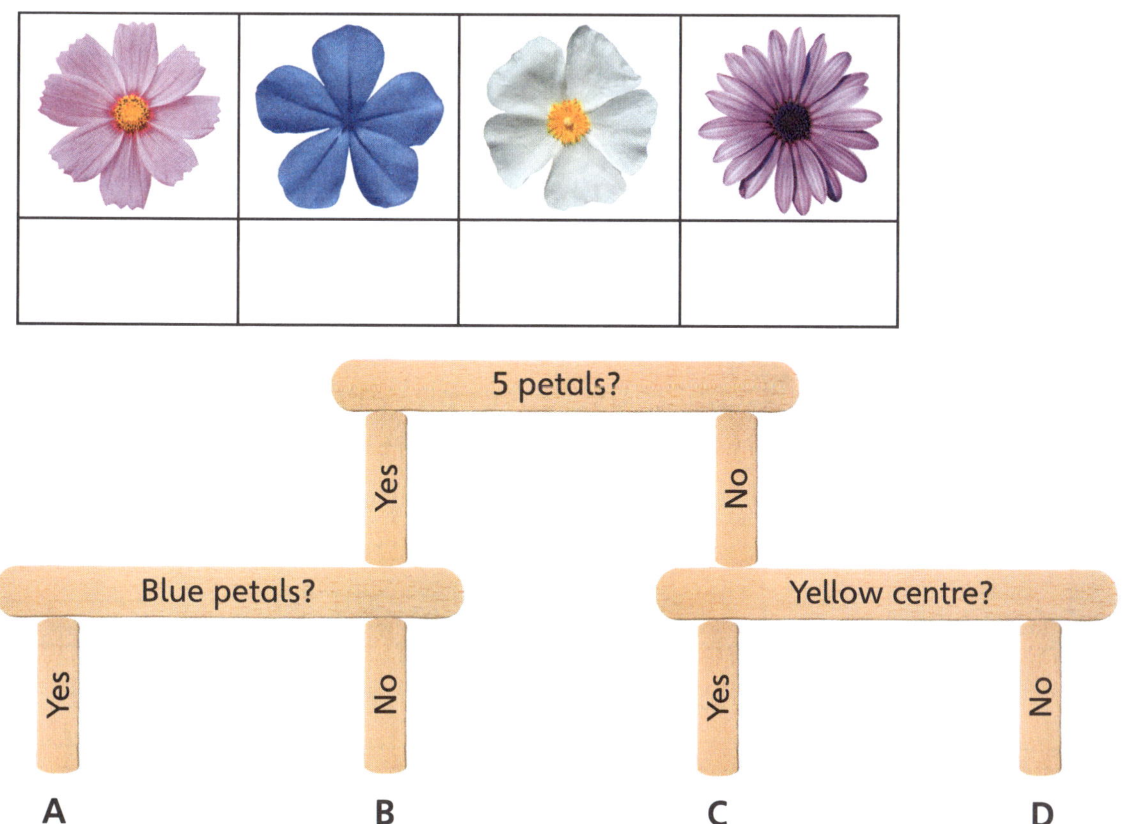

Revision: Growing plants

1 Complete the labels for the parts of this plant.

2 Write the name of **one** plant part beside each function.

You will write some plant parts more than once.

	anchors the plant in the soil
	attracts insects for pollination
	holds the leaves above the ground
	makes food using sunlight
	makes seeds for reproduction
	takes in water and minerals from the soil
	takes water from the roots to the leaves

3 Complete the labels for the parts of this tree.

4 Draw arrows to show the path of water as it **enters** this plant, **moves through it**, then **evaporates into the air**.

1 The picture shows two plants and their roots.

a)   Label the roots on both plants.

b)   Name **two** things that roots take from the soil.

1. ________________________   2. ________________________

c)   Describe the pattern of each plant's roots and why they are like this.

Plant A

Pattern of roots: ________________________

Reason: ________________________

____

Plant B

Pattern of roots: ________________________

Reason: ________________________

____

2 a) Circle the most likely position of the light source for these plants.

b) Why do plants need light?

____

3 Describe the **habitat** of these plants and how they are **adapted** to live there.

Plant	Description of habitat	Adaptations of plant

1 a)   What is happening to this bread?

____

b)   Which type of micro-organism made this bread change?

____

c)   Write **one other** way in which micro-organisms can be harmful.

____

2 a)   What do humans use yeast for?

____

b)   Which type of micro-organism is yeast? Circle **one** answer.

bacterium   microscopic fungus   virus

c)   Write **three other** ways in which micro-organisms can be useful.

1. _______________________________________

2. _______________________________________

3. _______________________________________

3 a)   Name the equipment used to observe micro-organisms.

____

b) Name the **two** types of micro-organism that are decomposers.

   1. ______________________   2. ______________________

c) Name **two** things that decomposers break down.

   1. ______________________   2. ______________________

4 **a)** Describe what each person is doing to prevent food poisoning.

b) **(i)** Why do we try to keep flies away from food?

   ____

   ____

(ii) Write **one** way to stop flies landing on food.

   ____

Revision: Plant life cycles

1 a) Complete the labels for the **six** parts of this flower.

b) Write the function of each of these parts of a flower.

anther	
petal	
nectary	
sepal	
stigma	

c) Write **three** ways in which a wind-pollinated flower differs from the one on this page.

1. ____

2. ____

3. ____

2 a) (i) Complete the labels for these parts of a flower.

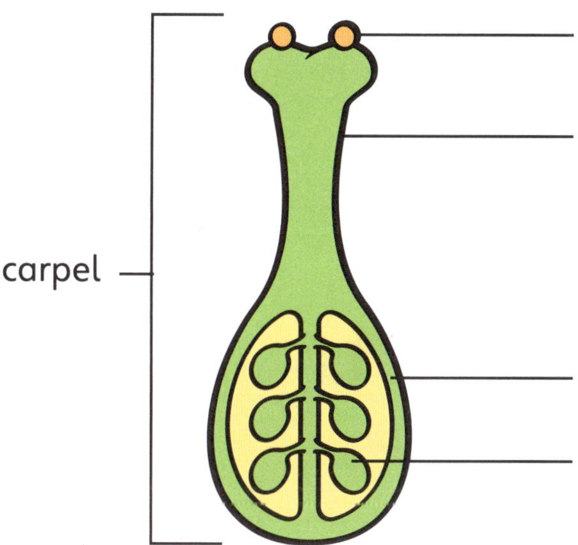

(ii) Circle the part of a plant's life cycle shown in part (i).

fertilisation   germination

pollination   seed dispersal

b) The nucleus of a pollen grain contains half the information to make a seed.

Where does it need to send this information?

____

3 Write the method of dispersal for each seed.

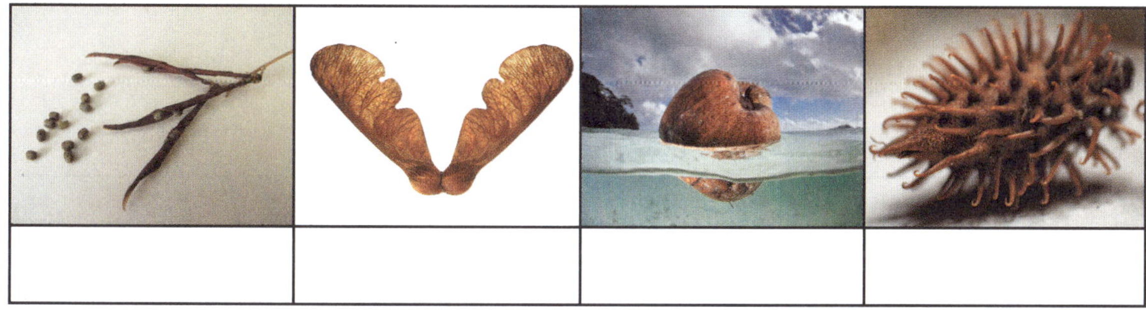

Revision: Heart, lungs and circulation

1 a) Label **heart**, **lung**, **rib**, **diaphragm** and **trachea**.

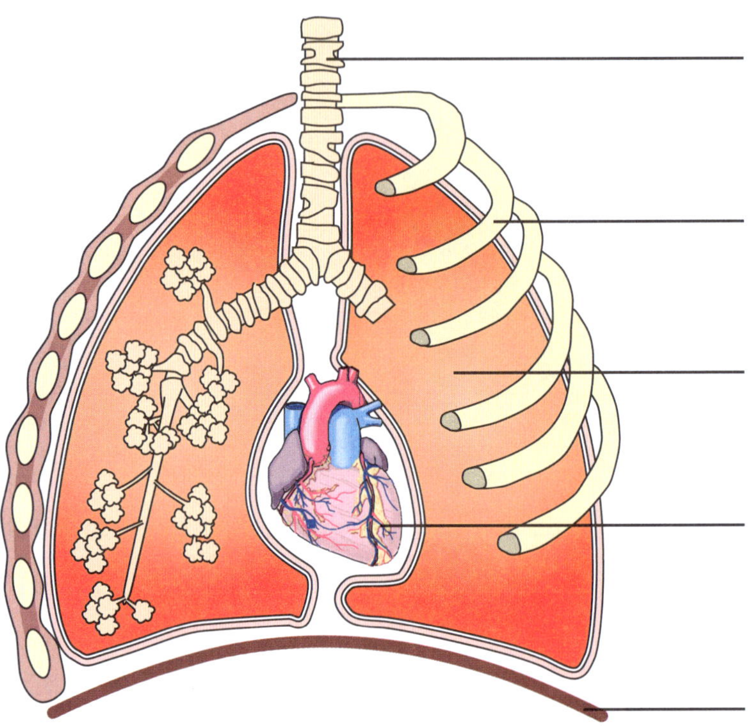

b) Write the function of each of these parts.

heart	
lungs	
ribs	

c) The heart and blood vessels are part of which body system?

____

2 The graph shows how pulse rate changes with exercise.

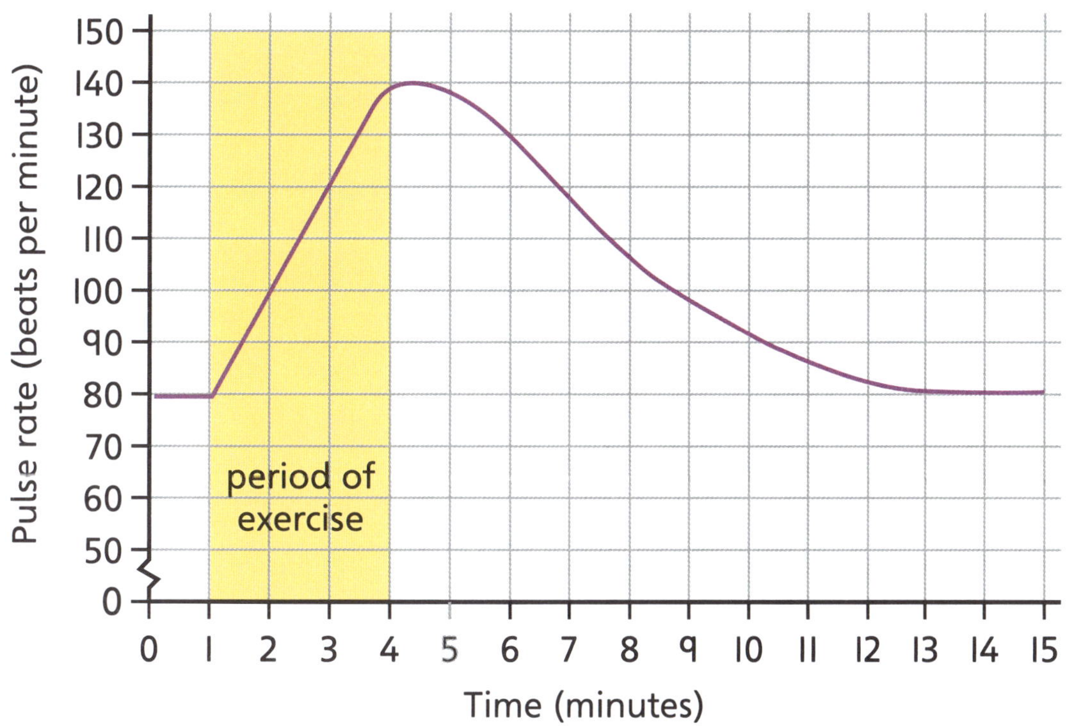

a) How long was the period of exercise?

____

b) What was the resting pulse rate? _______________________________

c) What was the highest pulse rate? _______________________________

d) At what time did the pulse rate return to its resting rate?

____

e) Explain why pulse rate increases when exercising.

____

____

____

Revision: Solids, liquids and gases

1 Write **solid**, **liquid** or **gas** beside each label.

2 Write **solid**, **liquid** or **gas** beside each statement.

Flows and can form a pool. _______________________

Holds its shape and does not flow. _______________________

Takes the shape of a container. _______________________

Moves easily and can escape from an unsealed container. _______________

3 a) Name the equipment used to measure temperature.

____

b) Write the unit for temperature. _______________________

c) What is temperature a measure of?

____

d) At what temperature does pure water boil and freeze?

boil: _______________ freeze: _______________

4 A learner incorrectly thinks that sand is a liquid.

Explain to the learner why they are wrong. Include a drawing if it helps you to explain.

____

____

____

____

____

Revision: Mixing and separating materials

1. Name the equipment used for separating shown in the pictures.

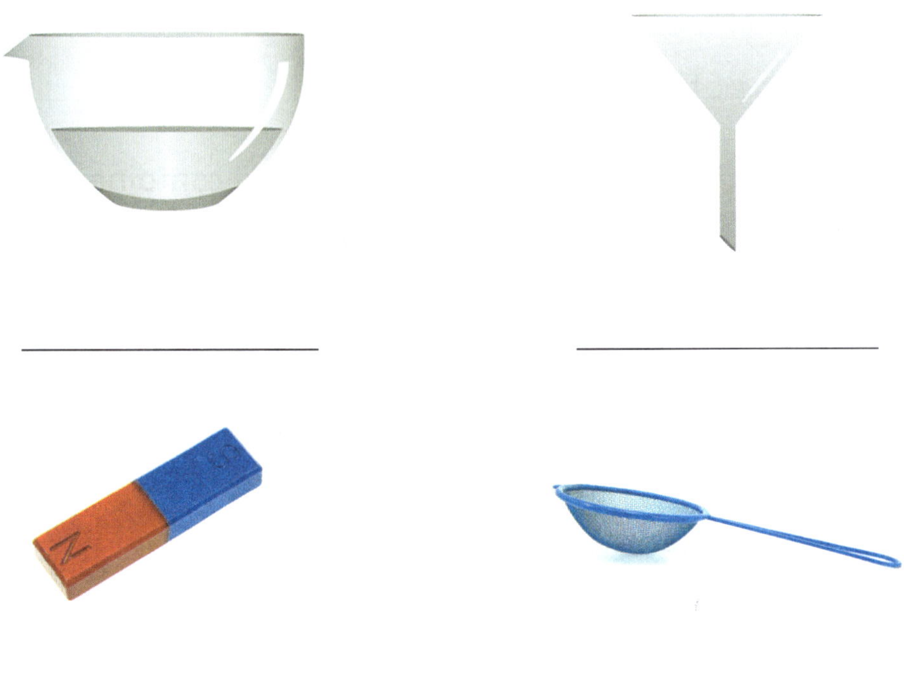

2. Put **one** tick (✓) in each row to show whether these substances are **soluble** or **insoluble**.

Substance	Soluble?	Insoluble?
sand		
salt		
sugar		
flour		

3. Write **three** ways to make a solute dissolve faster in a solvent.

1. ____

2. ____

3. ____

4 Complete the sentences about choosing a method of separating.

If one material is magnetic, use a ___________________.

If two solids have grains of different sizes, use a ___________________.

If there is a dissolved solid in a liquid, use ___________________.

If there is an insoluble solid in a liquid, use ___________________.

5 The graph shows how much of different solids dissolve in the same volume of water at different temperatures.

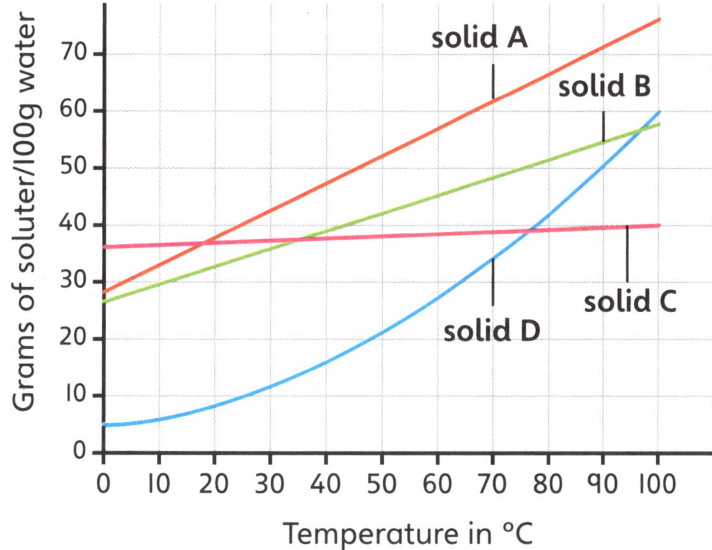

a)   How much of **solid B** dissolved at 10 °C? ___________________

b)   At what temperature did 40 g of **solid C** dissolve? ___________________

c)   (i)   Which solid did the change of temperature affect **most**?

____

(ii)   Which solid did the change of temperature affect **least**?

____

d)   At what temperature did the **same** mass of **solid A** and **solid C** dissolve? ___________________

1 a) Put **one** tick (✓) in each row to show whether the change is **reversible** or **irreversible**.

Change		Reversible?	Irreversible?
rusting			
melting			
evaporating			
burning			
baking bread			

b) Write **three** observations that show a change is **irreversible**.

1. ____

2. ____

3. ____

2 Write **evaporation**, **condensation**, **freezing** or **melting** on each arrow.

3 Write **solvent**, **solution** or **solute** under each picture.

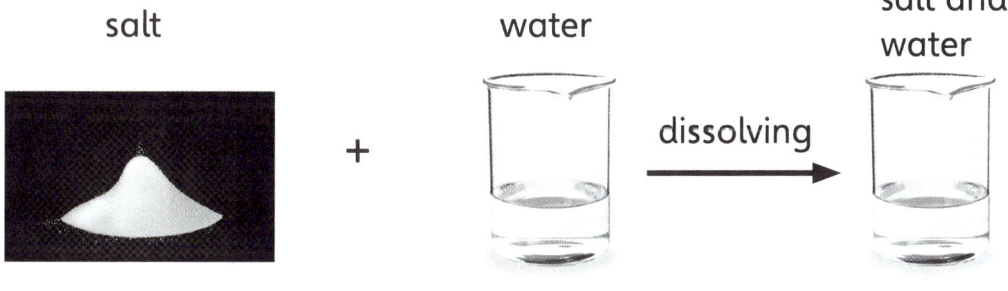

______________   ______________   ______________

4 Write labels for **sea**, **land**, **evaporation**, **condensation** and **precipitation** on the drawing of the water cycle.

Revision: Light

1. The picture shows a child trying to make an animal shape with her hands.

   Use the letters on the picture to answer the questions.

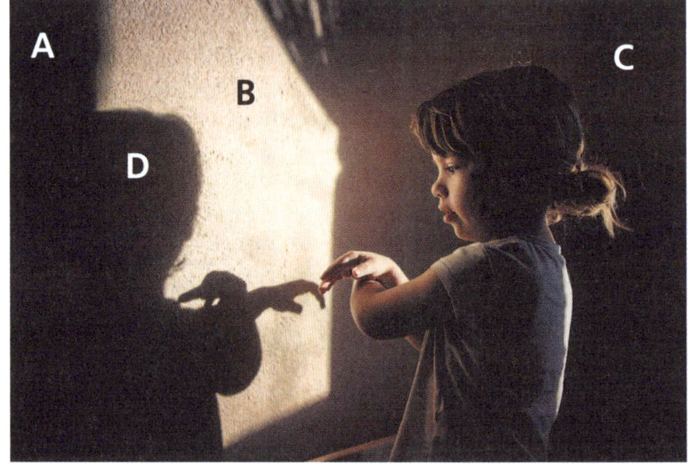

   a) Write **light** or **dark** beside each letter below.

   A ________________________   B ________________________

   C ________________________   D ________________________

   b) Which letter shows a **shadow**?

   ____

2. Put a tick (✓) under all the **sources** of light.

3 Complete the sentences about shadows.

A shadow is formed when light from a source is _________________ by

an _________________ object.

The shadow is the same _________________ as the object but might

not be the same _________________.

4 The picture shows the shadow of a football on a flat surface.

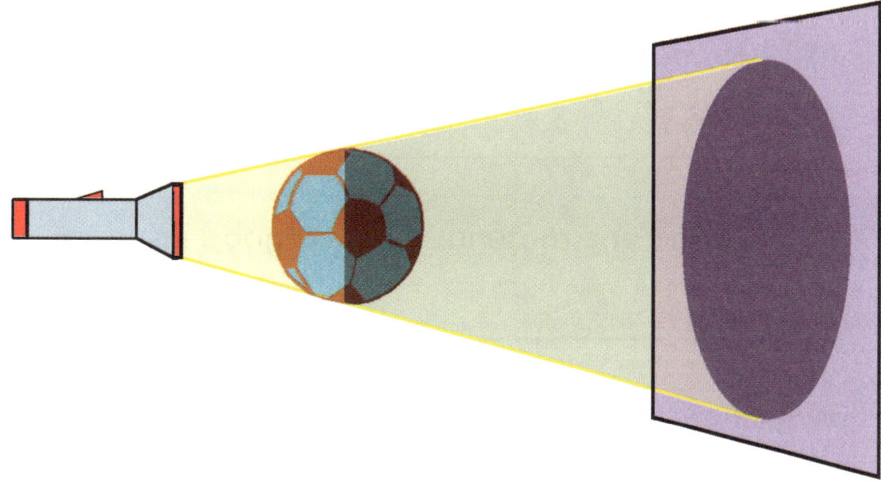

a)   Label **football**, **light source** and **flat surface** on the diagram.

b)   (i)   Suggest how to make the shadow **bigger**.

      ____

      (ii)   Suggest how to make the shadow **smaller**.

      ____

c)   Write **two** words, **both ending in -er**, to complete this sentence
      about shadow sizes.

      The _________________ the opaque object is to the light source,

      the _________________ the size of the shadow.

1 a) Label **conductor** and **insulator** on this picture.

b) (i) Name **one** material that is a good conductor.

____

(ii) Name **one** material that is a good insulator.

____

c) Write **two** ways in which mains electricity is dangerous.

1. ____

2. ____

2 a) Name **two** kitchen appliances that use **mains** electricity.

1. ____________________ 2. ____________________

b) Name **two** devices that can use batteries.

1. ____________________ 2. ____________________

3 a) What is a **switch** used for in a circuit?

____

b) What is the function of a **cell** in a circuit?

____

4 a) The bulb does **not** light in this circuit. Explain why.

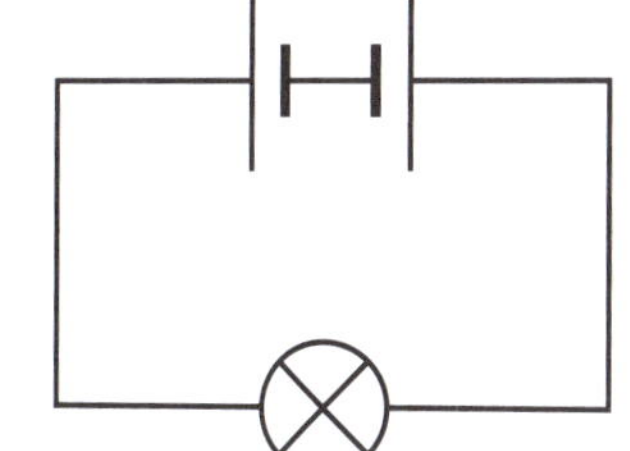

____

b) Redraw this circuit so that the bulb lights.

5 The bulb does **not** light in this circuit. Explain why.

____

____

6 In this circuit, both bulbs are lit.

a) Bulb **B** breaks.

Predict what happens to bulb **A**.

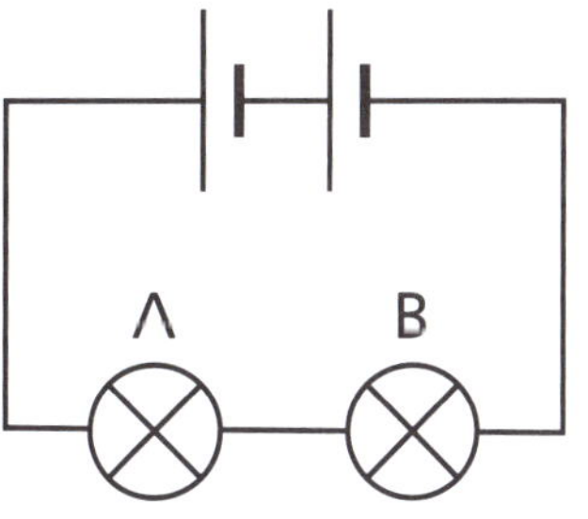

____

b) Explain the reason for your answer to a).

____

____

1 a) Put **one** tick (✓) in each row to show whether the object is a **source of light** or **reflects light**.

Object	Source of light?	Reflects light?
candle		
diamond		
street lamps		
Sun		

b) The picture shows the Moon and the sea at night.

(i) Explain why the Moon looks bright.

____

____

(ii) Explain why the sea looks bright.

____

____

2 The table shows the definitions of three scientific words.
Write the **three** missing words.

A material that blocks light.	
You can see clearly through this material because it lets lots of light through.	
You cannot see clearly through this material because it only lets some light through.	

3 Draw the reflected ray. Use a ruler and show the direction.

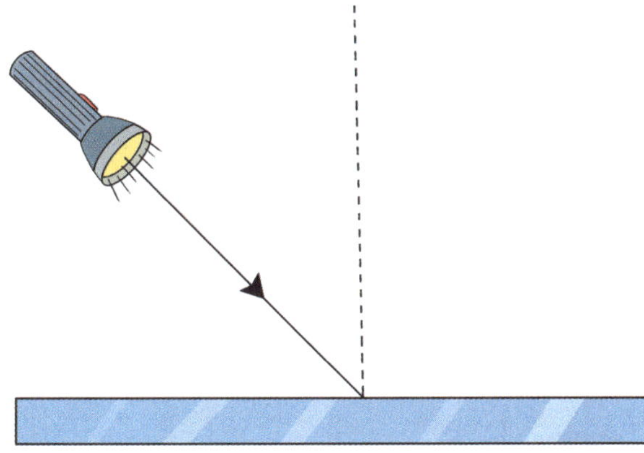
shiny surface

4 Draw a ray diagram to show how light from the lamp helps the cat to see the bird.
Use a ruler. Remember to show the direction in which light travels.

Revision: Electricity: Changing circuits

1 Complete the table by:

a) naming each component
b) drawing the circuit symbol.

Component	Name of component	Symbol
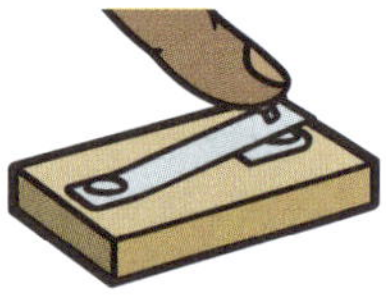		
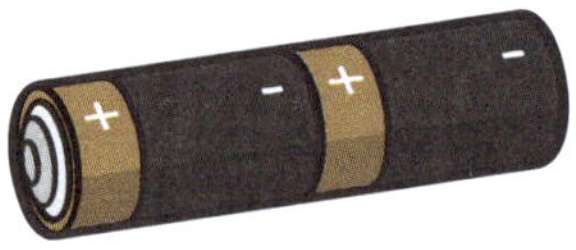		
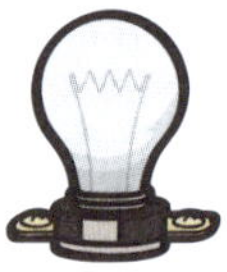		
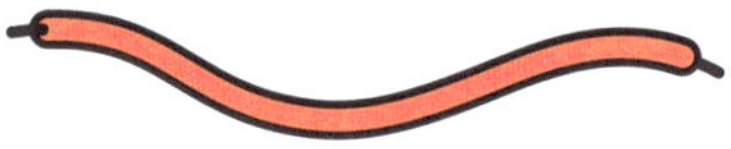		
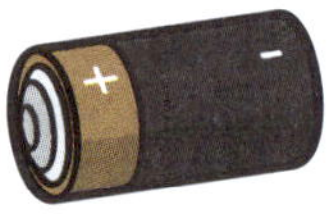		
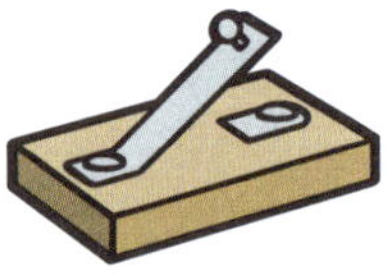		
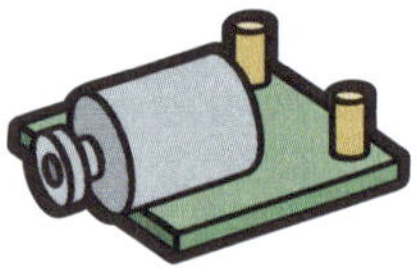		
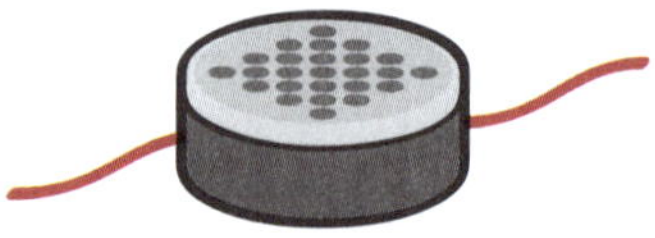		

2 **a)** Explain why the bulb in circuit **B** is brighter than the bulb in circuit **A**.

A   B

normal brightness   brighter

____

____

b) **(i)** Predict what will happen if another bulb is added to circuit **A**.

____

(ii) Predict what will happen if another bulb is added to circuit **B**.

____

3 **a)** Use symbols to draw a circuit with two cells, a closed switch and a buzzer.

b) Draw **two** different circuits in which the buzzer is **quieter**, but still makes a sound.

1 Complete the sentences about space.

The Sun is a __________________.

The Sun is at the centre of our __________________ __________________.

Earth is a __________________ with one __________________ orbiting it.

Earth and the other __________________ orbit the __________________.

2 The drawing shows nine objects in space.

a) Name the **nine** objects.

1. __________________   2. __________________

3. __________________   4. __________________

5. __________________   6. __________________

7. __________________   8. __________________

9. __________________

b) What do the eight dotted lines (▮ ▮) represent?

____

3 This is an old model of the Solar System.

Write **two** ways in which this model differs from the modern one shown in question 2.

1. ____

2. ____

4 a) Complete the pictures so that each one shows **the Sun** and a **shadow** of the tree.

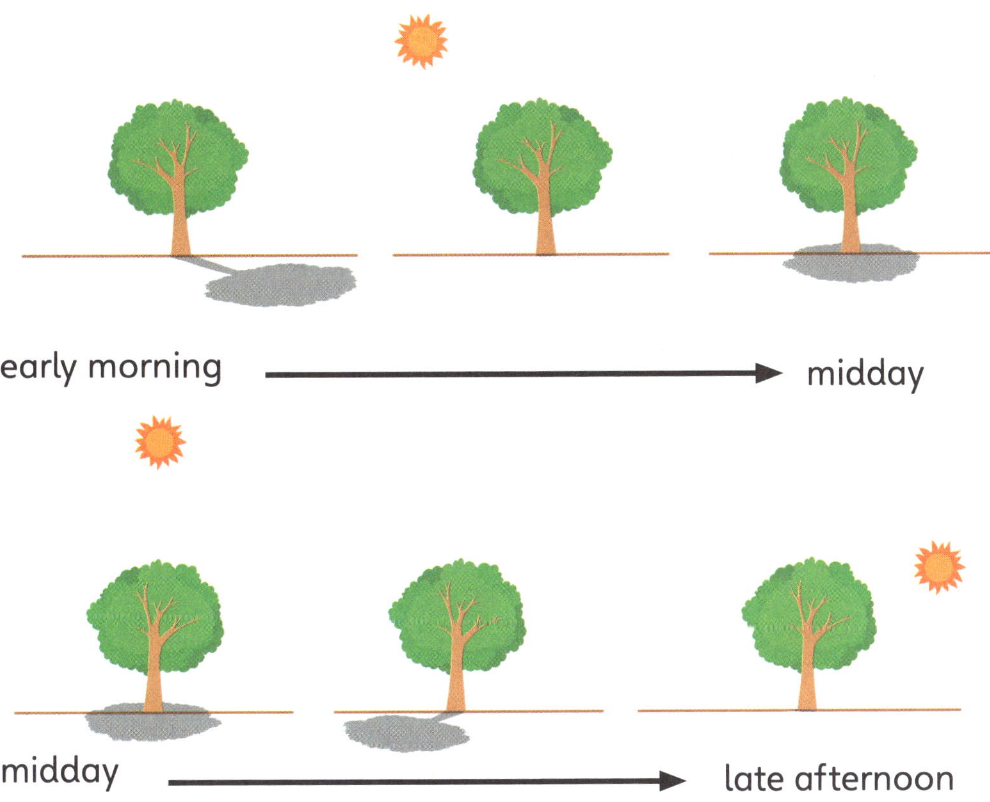

b) The Sun does not revolve around Earth. Explain why it is in a different place in each picture.

____

____

Revision: Forces in air and water

1 a) Name this equipment, which is used to measure forces. _______________

b) What is the weight of the apple? _______________ N

c) What unit does N represent? _______________

2 a) The force of gravity is a *non-contact force*.
What does this mean? _______________

____

b) Complete the sentence.

The force of gravity acts between the _______________ and a falling object.

3 a) This car has snow chains.

Which force do snow chains affect and how?
Tick (✓) **one** box.

they decrease air resistance	
they increase friction	
they decrease weight	
they increase water resistance	

b) Which force makes this tennis ball fall to the ground?
Tick (✓) **one** box.

gravity		air resistance	
friction		water resistance	

4 a) Circle the most streamlined vehicle.

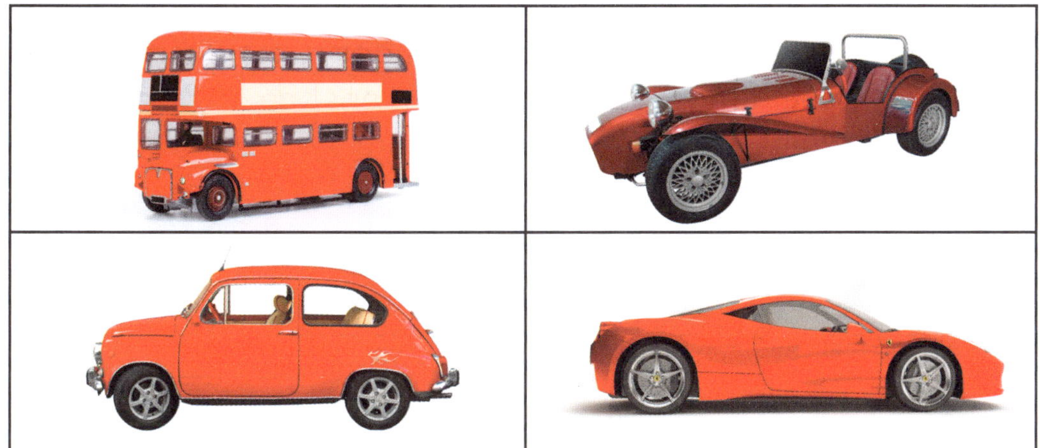

b) Name **one** force that streamlining reduces. ___________________

5 This truck is driving forwards on a flat road.

a) Draw **one** force arrow to show the **weight** of the truck.
Label it **W**.

b) (i) Name **two** forces that are **slowing** the truck.

I. ___________________ 2. ___________________

(ii) Draw force arrows on the picture to show where **each** of
the slowing forces acts.

1 Abi wants to find out about how sugar cubes dissolve in water. Write **three** different scientific questions she could answer by doing an investigation.

1. ____

____

2. ____

____

3. ____

____

2 Plan an investigation to find out whether changing the temperature of the water affects the time taken for a sugar cube to dissolve.

a) Write a scientific question for this investigation.

____

____

b) Put **one** tick (✓) in each row to show what to do for each variable.

Variable	Change?	Measure?	Keep the same?
number of stirs			
temperature of the water			
size of sugar cubes			
time for sugar to dissolve			
volume of water used			
number of sugar cubes			

c)   Why are some variables kept the same each time?

____

d)   How will you know when to take your measurement each time?

____

____

3 List the equipment you will need and draw a labelled scientific diagram of it set up and ready to start.

____

____

____

____

____

____

____

4 Write the column headings for a results table.

5 What can you do to make your results more reliable?

____

Revision: Conclusions and evaluation of evidence

1 A class make this bar chart to show their favourite pet.

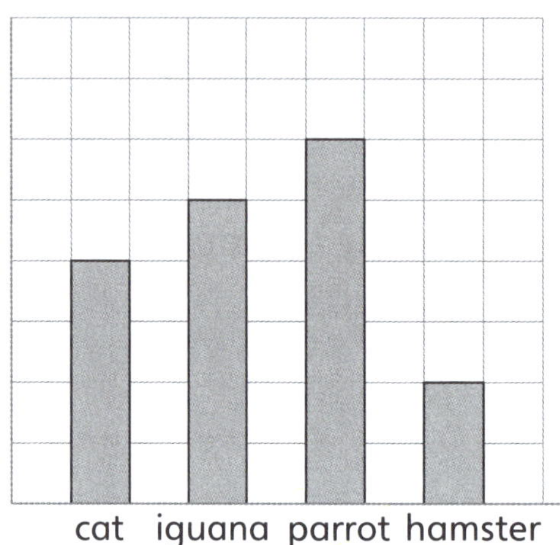

a) (i)   **Four** learners chose **cat** as their favourite pet. Use this information to number the vertical axis of the bar chart.

(ii)   Write axis labels for **both** axes.

b)   How many learners did the class ask in total?

2 This graph shows how the temperature of a beaker of water changes.

a) At what time was the temperature 30 °C?

____

b) Describe what the results show.

____

____

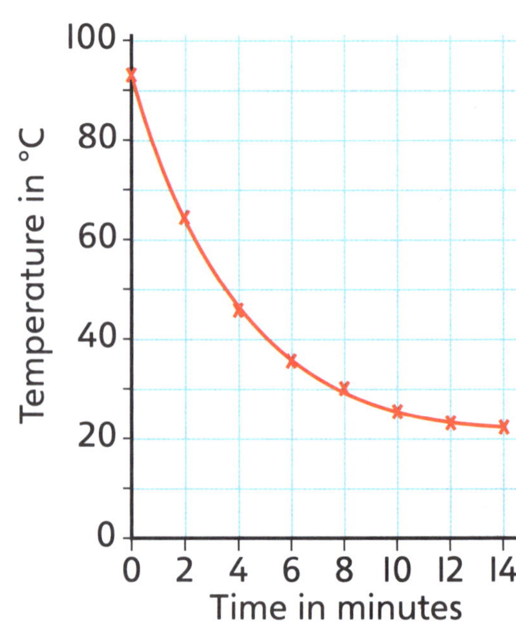

3 The graph shows the mass of a solid that dissolves in 100 cm³ of water at different temperatures.

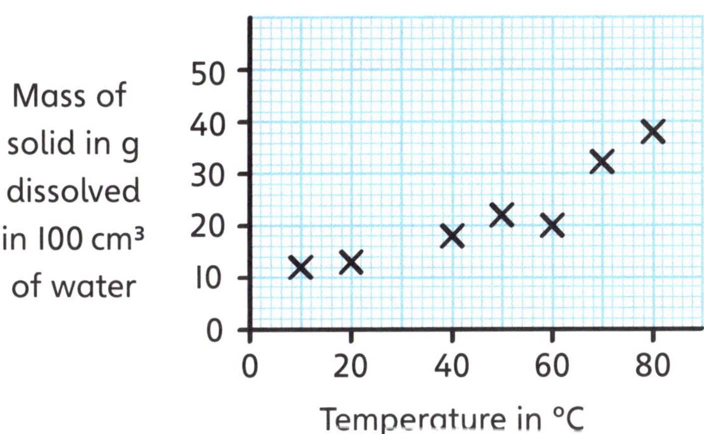

a) Describe the pattern shown by the results.

____

____

b) (i) Circle **one** result that does not fit the pattern.

(ii) Do you think this result is too high or too low?

____

(iii) Suggest something that the learner could have done wrong to get this result.

____

c) Predict the mass of solid that dissolves at 30 °C. ______________

d) Suggest a way to improve the reliability of the results.

____

How is my learning tested?

 I understand that command words in tests and examinations are words that tell me what to do.

I know this because I can think of a short question that starts with each of these command words.

Command word	Example of a short question using the word
Add to	
Circle	
Complete	
Describe	
Draw	
Explain	
Give	
Name	
Plot	
Predict	
State	
Tick	

2 I understand the units needed for measurements in science.

I know this because I can write **length**, **temperature**, **volume**, **area**, **time**, **force**, **speed** or **mass** beside each group of units.

I also know this because I can write **the name of one piece of equipment that has these units on it**.

Group of units	Used when measuring	Equipment using these units
millimetres (mm) centimetres (cm) metres (m) kilometres (km)		
square centimetres (cm²) square metres (m²)		graph paper
cubic centimetres (cm³) cubic decimetres (dm³) litres (l) millilitres (ml)	volume	
grams (g) kilograms (kg)		
newtons (N)		
seconds (s) minutes (min) hours (h)		
metres per second (m/s) kilometres per hour (km/h)		speedometer
degrees Celsius (°C)		

(key: b-bottom; c-centre; l-left; r-right; t-top)

Non-Prominent Image Credit(s):

123RF GB LIMITED: anetagu 68c, berlinimpressions 10 L-R 2t, 120 L-R 2t, Darren Pullman 29 T-B 4, Dmitry Rukhlenko 136 T-B 2t, Jakub Gojda 130 T-B 2, nenovbrothers 69t, pakete 62t, Luo Hongzhi 64t; **ALAMY IMAGES:** Deefish T-B 5, Sciencephotos 63 T-B 2t; **GETTY IMAGES INCORPORATED:** laymul/iStock 82t, laymul/iStock 94t, blueringmedia/iStock 118t; **PEARSON EDUCATION:** Amit John 131b, Arvind Singh Negi/Red Reef Design Studio 117b, Cheuk-king Lo 68 L T-B 2t, Coleman Yuen 61 T-B 4, 62t, Gareth Boden 71 T-B 1, HL Studios 94b, 95t, Joey Chan/Pearson Education Asia Ltd 4t, Mohammed Ali 56t, 99c, Mohammed Ali 133, Mohd Suhail 122t, 64 T-B 1c, 64b, 44 L-R 1t, 30t, Oxford Designers & Illustrators Ltd 56b, 58t, 101c, 101t, 112t, 87c, 95 L-R 1c, PDQ Digital Media Solutions Ltd 53t, 109 L-R 1c, 109 L-R 2c, 109 L-R 3c, 113t, 116t, 146t, 147b, 86 L-R 1b, 86 L-R 2b, 80c, Pearson Education Ltd 102 R, 124, 125, 146b, 44b, 45, Ratan Mani Banerjee 38t, 44 L-R 2t, 44 L-R 3t, 52 L-R 1t, 52 L-R 2t, 52 L-R 3t, 52 L-R 4t, Trevor Clifford 59 L-R 1c, Tsz-shan Kwok 102 T-B 5t; **SCIENCE PHOTO LIBRARY:** TREVOR CLIFFORD PHOTOGRAPHY 61 T-B 1, 61 T-B 2, 61 T-B 3, 61 T-B 5, MARTYN F. CHILLMAID 89t, SCIENCE PHOTO LIBRARY 142t; **SHUTTERSTOCK:** 543709 83, A Daily Odyssey/Shutterstcok 29 T-B 2, 123 L-R 4b, aekikuis. 141b, Aldona Griskeviciene 94c, Aleksei Kochev 132 L-R 2b, AlessandroZocc 29 T-B 3, Ali DM 48, Amanda Carden 136 T-B 4t, Andrey_Popov 8b, Andrii Bezvershenko 7 L-R 1t, 7 L-R 2t, Anest 119t, Anthony Pham 26 T-B 5, anthonycz 77t, April stock 115 L-R 1b, Billion Photos 62t, Birgit Reitz-Hofmann 14t, Blamb 38b, Blue bee. 140c, BlueRingMedia 103b, 14, 74b, 75t, 76c, Car n food designer 90t, carroteater 6c, Cozine 62t, DariaBumblebee 75c, Denny Davidson 141, denysganbaphotography 68 R T-B 1t, Designua 66b, 66t, 67c, 67t, Dragon Images 121 T-B 3, efiplus 143 L T-B 2t, Ekramar 70c, Electrical Engineer 102 T-B 3t, Eric Isselee. 137 L-R 3b, Erkki Makkonen 115c, Ethan Daniels 123 L-R 3b, 29 T-B 1, eva_blanco 130 T-B 5, Ewa Studio 137 L-R 1b, FabrikaSimf 121 T-B 1, Fedorov Ivan Sergeevich 84t, Fotokostic 69c, GraphicsRF.com 102 T-B 2t, 102 T-B 4t, 32, 99b, Halfpoint 4b, Havryliuk-Kharzhevska 117t, Heike Rau 123 L-R 1b, Hennadii H 14 L-R 4c, Hong Vo 26 T-B 3, huntingSHARK 102b, 103c, 103t, 108b, 98t, Igor Klyakhin 26 T-B 2, Imageman 22b, Ingrid Prats. 136b, Intarapong 88t, Jade ThaiCatwalk 126c, Jaroslav Moravcik 142c, JCLobo. 136 T-B 1t, Jenson 88t, Jerry Gantar 2lb, jessicahyde 26 T-B 4, Joe Gough 62t, johavel 143c, jokerpro 136 T-B 3t, Karamelity 70 L-R 1t, Kazakova Maryia 28b, Kei Shooting 130 T-B 3, 68 L T-B 1t, Kitch Bain 88t, Kopirin 14 L-R 3c, Kuttelvaserova Stuchelova 10 L-R 1t, 120 L-R 1t, Lazy_Bear 132 L-R 1b, Leremy 128 L T-B 1t, 128 R T-B 1t, 98 L-R 1b, 98 L-R 2b, 98 L-R 3b, Lisa-S 8 T-B 2t, LorraineHudgins 29 T-B 6, m.malinika 15c, Marek Hajdukiewicz 13t, Margo Harrison 90 L-R 1b, Marie Shark 33 L-R 1b, Marijus Auruskevicius 132 L-R 3b, Maryna Shymkovych 132t, Max Topchii 119 T-B 4b, mbarredo 119 T-B 3b, medvedsky.kz 143 R T-B 2t, MeKaDesign 46, 47, Mindscape studio 59 L-R 2c, Modvector 62c, Nadezhda Nesterova 20t, Nathanael Siders 24t, Net Vector 65, New Africa 131c, 60t, Nil Kulp 88 T-B 4b, NIPAPORN PANYACHAROEN 33 L-R 2t, Nowwy Jirawat 70 L-R 2t, Oleg Elkov 130 T-B 4, Olga Aniven 88 T-B 1b, Olga_Narcissa 65t, Pabkov 8 T-B 1t, Pedro Turrini Neto 23, petrroudny43 65, photostar72 143 R T-B 1t, Pitsanu Kraichana 71 T-B 3, Piyaphat Detbun 33 L-R 2b, ppl 114b, PRILL 28t, Prixel Creative 88 T-B 3b, ProStockStudio/Shutterwstock 121 T-B 2, QBR 68 R T-B 1t, Quang Ho 26 T-B 1, Rak ter samer 115 L-R 2b, Rawpixel.com 86t, Ray49 123 L-R 2b, Reamolko. 137 L-R 2b, redknapper 128 L T-B 2t, renklerin kafasi 137c, RG-vc 143 L T-B 1t, Richard Peterson 128 R T-B 2t, Ropsie Chids 57t, Rose Carson 62t, Rostislav Stefanek 119 T-B 2b, RukiMedia 84c, Rvector 87b, 95 L-R 2c, S_Photo 64 T-B 2c, saengdao 33 L-R 1t, Scharfsinn 90 L-R 2b, Shutter Baby photo 88t, steshs 33 L-R 1c, Studio Barcelona 119t, studiovin 126c, Suzanne Tucker 71 T-B 2, szefei 20b, TADDEUS 134t, TamuT 8c, tawanroong 15t, TippaPatt 115 L-R 4b, tr3gin 115 L-R 3b, udaix 34b, Usova Olga 98 L-R 1c, 98 L-R 2c, UzFoto 88 T-B 2b, Vaclav Sebek 119 T-B 1b, Vecton 38c, VectorMine 40, 50c, Vectorpocket 14 L-R 2c, vfpictures 56c, Viktoria Bykova 9, vinz89 82b, vitaliyborkovskiy 33 L-R 2c, Volodymyr Nikitenko 130 T-B 1, 68b, WICHAI WONGJONGJAIHAN 142b, Wirestock Creators 57c, world of vector 43, yusufdemirci 80b, Zelfit 132 L-R 4b.

All other images © Pearson Education